Foreign Policy
and the Constitution

A DECADE OF STUDY OF THE CONSTITUTION

How Democratic Is the Constitution?

Robert A. Goldwin and William A. Schambra, editors

How Capitalistic Is the Constitution?

Robert A. Goldwin and William A. Schambra, editors

How Does the Constitution Secure Rights?

Robert A. Goldwin and William A. Schambra, editors

Separation of Powers: Does It Still Work?

Robert A. Goldwin and Art Kaufman, editors

How Federal Is the Constitution?

Robert A. Goldwin and William A. Schambra, editors

How Does the Constitution Protect Religious Freedom?

Robert A. Goldwin and Art Kaufman, editors

Slavery and Its Consequences:
The Constitution, Equality, and Race

Robert A. Goldwin and Art Kaufman, editors

The Constitution, the Courts, and the Quest for Justice

Robert A. Goldwin and William A. Schambra, editors

Foreign Policy and the Constitution

Robert A. Goldwin and Robert A. Licht, editors

Foreign Policy and the Constitution

*Robert A. Goldwin
and Robert A. Licht,*
editors

The AEI Press
Publisher for the American Enterprise Institute
Washington, D.C.

This book is the ninth in a series in AEI's project "A Decade of Study of the Constitution," funded in part by grants from the National Endowment for the Humanities. A full list of the titles appears on the series page.

Distributed by arrangement with

University Press of America, Inc.
4720 Boston Way   3 Henrietta Street
Lanham, MD 20706   London WC2E 8LU England

Library of Congress Cataloging-in-Publication Data

Foreign policy and the Constitution / edited by Robert A. Goldwin and
   Robert A. Licht.
      p.   cm.
   ISBN 0-8447-3721-6 (alk. paper).—ISBN 0-8447-3722-4 (pbk. :
alk. paper)
      1. United States—Foreign relations—Law and legislation—
Congresses.   2. United States—Foreign relations administration—
Congresses.   3. Separation of powers—United States—Congresses.
I. Goldwin, Robert A., 1922–   .   II. Licht, Robert A.
KF4651.A5F67   1990
342.73'0412—dc20
[347.302412]   89-18448
                                                          CIP

1 3 5 7 9 10 8 6 4 2

AEI Studies 507

The AEI Press
Publisher for the American Enterprise Institute
1150 Seventeenth Street, N.W., Washington, D.C. 20036

Printed in the United States of America

Contents

The Editors and the Authors

ROBERT A. GOLDWIN is resident scholar and director of constitutional studies at the American Enterprise Institute. He served in the White House as special consultant to the president of the United States and, concurrently, as adviser to the secretary of defense. He has taught at the University of Chicago and Kenyon College and was dean of St. John's College in Annapolis. He is the editor or coeditor of more than a score of books, including *How Democratic Is the Constitution?*, *How Capitalistic Is the Constitution?*, *How Does the Constitution Secure Rights?*, and *How Federal Is the Constitution?*, and is the author of *Why Blacks, Women, and Jews Are Not Mentioned in the Constitution, and Other Unorthodox Views*.

ROBERT A. LICHT is associate director of constitutional studies at the American Enterprise Institute. Mr. Licht taught philosophy at Bucknell University and liberal arts at St. John's College in Annapolis. He has been a visiting scholar at the Kennedy Institute for Ethics and a National Endowment for the Humanities Fellow at AEI. At *U.S. News and World Report*, Mr. Licht was assistant to the president, assistant to the publisher, and senior editor of the book division. He is the author of "On the Three Parties in America" and "Reflections on Martin Diamond's 'Ethics and Politics: The American Way.'"

MARK BLITZ is director of political and social studies and senior research fellow at the Hudson Institute. At the U.S. Information Agency, he was associate director, head of the Bureau of Educational and Cultural Affairs, and director of Private Sector Programs. Mr. Blitz was a senior staff member of the U.S. Senate Committee on Foreign Relations and with ACTION. He was a professor at Harvard University and the University of Pennsylvania. Mr. Blitz is the author of *Heidegger's "Being and Time" and the Possibility of Political Philosophy* and several articles on political philosophy and foreign affairs.

DICK CHENEY, secretary of defense, was, at the time of writing, a member of Congress (at large) from Wyoming (since 1978) and the newly elected Republican whip for the 101st Congress. His congressional experience includes positions as chairman of the House Republican Policy Committee and the House Republican Conference, and he served on the House Committee on Interior and Insular Affairs, House Permanent Select Committee on Intelligence, and House Select Committee to Investigate Covert Arms Transactions with Iran. Mr. Cheney was White House chief of staff under President Ford.

JACQUES J. GORLIN is a consulting economist in Washington, D.C. Mr. Gorlin served in a number of senior positions in both the executive and legislative branches of government, including the Treasury Department, the Office of the U.S. Trade Representative, the State Department, and the Agency for International Development, and was senior economic adviser to Senator Jacob Javits. Mr. Gorlin has lectured and written extensively about economics, particularly international trade, finance, and economic development.

EDMUND S. MUSKIE is a senior partner with Chadbourne & Parke, an international law firm in Washington, D.C. Mr. Muskie served three terms in the Maine legislature, served as governor of Maine from 1954 to 1958, and was a U.S. senator for twenty-two years, until his appointment as secretary of state in 1980.

JACK N. RAKOVE is professor of history and director of the American studies program at Stanford University. He is the author of *The Beginnings of National Politics: An Interpretive History of the Continental Congress* and numerous articles on constitutional history and politics.

NATHAN TARCOV, professor of political science at the University of Chicago, recently served as secretary of the Navy research fellow at the U.S. Naval War College. He was a member of the policy planning staff at the U.S. Department of State. Mr. Tarcov has written extensively on political theory, American political thought, and American foreign policy and is the author of *Locke's Education for Liberty*.

MICHAEL M. UHLMANN is a partner in the Washington office of Pepper, Hamilton & Scheetz. Mr. Uhlmann was special assistant to President Ronald Reagan for nearly four years. He also served as associate director of the White House Office of Policy Development and executive secretary to the Cabinet Council on Legal Policy. He has held staff positions in the Senate, Federal Trade Commission, and Department of Justice. Mr. Uhlmann has written numerous articles on law and public policy.

Preface

Where does the Constitution lodge the power to determine the foreign relations of the United States? That question, as current as every new congressional session and as old as the Republic itself, is the subject dealt with in all the essays in this volume.

The Constitution gives to the Congress, and especially to the Senate, a prominent role in the conduct of foreign policy, and that has led to endless disputes. The argument on one side is that the nation is safer because there is a powerful legislative restraint on the executive branch. The argument on the other side is that legislative meddling interferes with the secrecy and decisiveness essential to formulating and carrying out a great power's diplomatic, military, and economic policies.

The separation of powers established by the Constitution is pervasive; consequently in much of the conduct of government, citizens and elected officials alike often find themselves asking who is in charge. In the conduct of foreign policy especially, persistent problems stem directly from the provisions of the Constitution dealing with the most important foreign policy powers: war and peace, the disposition of armed forces, and relations with allies and adversaries.

If the only problem were that the original provisions leave unclear who has responsibility for what, we could have remedied the defect by amendment at any time in the last two hundred years. The Twelfth Amendment, for example, was just such a correction of an unanticipated flaw in the procedures of the electoral college. But the kinds of issues that have caused so much trouble—the war powers, covert operations, secret negotiations, treaty ratifications, executive agreements, deployment of troops or ships—have never been "corrected" by amending any of the constitutional provisions. Why not? Why are we still perplexed by the same question—where does the Constitution lodge the power to determine our foreign policy?—that was hotly debated in the administration of President George Washington?

There is no way to keep the problem from coming up again and again because it may be inherent in a constitutional system of separation of powers. The problem certainly does not occur in anything like the same form in parliamentary systems. The reason it has persisted is suggested by the theoretical explanation provided by John Locke, one of the first proponents of separation of powers. Locke argued that in addition to the legislative power and the executive power there is a third power, which he called the federative power and which we can call the foreign policy power. If the legislative power is essentially a power to make laws and the executive power essentially to enforce the laws, then the foreign policy power, Locke argued, is neither legislative nor executive. This third power, though not executive in nature, Locke said, is nevertheless better left in the hands of the executive (for reasons set out fully in the essay by Nathan Tarcov).

When Locke wrote, no government had ever separated the legislative and executive branches in the manner and to the extent established by the Constitution of the United States; Locke did not have the opportunity to see the separation in practice. But he was well aware of innumerable examples of monarchical adventurism and the dangers of executive prerogative unrestrained by legislative power. In Locke's time the power to conduct foreign policy was commonly accepted as an inherent part of the executive power. His formulation that the foreign policy power is neither executive nor legislative would enable one to forecast our situation, a persistent and energetic competition in which both branches seek to control as much as possible of this important part of governmental power that doesn't naturally belong to either. In sum, the problem may be inherent in our system and therefore repeatedly the subject of prudential deliberation and political jockeying in every session of Congress and in every administration, no matter how clearly the constitutional provisions may be worded.

One foreign policy provision in the Constitution is unambiguously clear. The commerce clause gives to Congress, without qualifications, the power "to regulate commerce with foreign nations." If it were just a matter of clear wording in the Constitution, then there should be no difficulty in knowing where the power is lodged with respect to foreign trade. And yet Congress has found it necessary to delegate much of this power over foreign commerce to the executive branch; in the process, nevertheless, the same kinds of struggles occur as in every other part of the conduct of foreign policy. As evidence of the tension, Jacques Gorlin points out in his essay that the president, in signing the trade act of 1988, complained that parts of it were inconsistent with constitutional principles and that the Congress seemed to be seeking "to reduce [his] trade powers and to reassert its constitutional authority to regulate foreign commerce."

Apparently even a clear and unambiguous clause in the Constitution cannot prevent the struggle between the Congress and the president for control of foreign policy, or answer definitively the question of who is in charge.

Other essays in this volume examine two related questions: first, whether the tension between the legislative and executive branches is a direct consequence of the design of the Constitution, which determines their respective characteristics, and second, whether the Supreme Court has a decisive role in determining "where the power is lodged" when the tension between the other two branches brings the dispute before the courts.

What is clearest in all this uncertainty is the framers' concern about the powerful human tendency of government officials to act on their own, free of restraint from public opinion and the institutions accountable to the public. Examples of such official behavior abound in American political history right down to the present moment. For a variety of reasons, this tendency has always been regarded as most dangerous in the conduct of foreign policy. The framers were reluctant, as a result, to assign the foreign policy powers wholly to the executive, although they were acutely aware of the advantages of "a single voice" speaking for the nation in dealings with other nations. The same view of human nature, however, made them just as reluctant to assign unrestrained foreign policy powers to the Senate.

It is not surprising, therefore, that experienced public officials agree on the necessity for coordination and cooperation between the Congress and the executive branch for the effective conduct of foreign affairs. The last two essays—a debate between Edmund Muskie and Dick Cheney, two leaders with broad experience in executive and legislative positions—present forceful opposing views on the proper role of the executive and legislative branches. Mr. Muskie was governor of Maine before being elected to several terms in the Senate, followed by service as secretary of state. Mr. Cheney was White House chief of staff before being elected to several terms in the House of Representatives, followed by appointment as secretary of defense. (His essay was completed while he was still minority whip in the House, before his nomination to the executive branch.)

On the basis of their extensive experience, they agree on the need for coordination and cooperation between the two branches but disagree strongly on how to achieve the best combination of prudent executive decisiveness and constructive legislative oversight in critical activities such as covert operations, the exercise of war powers, and secret diplomatic negotiations.

We end with the question with which we began. As our representative constitutional democratic government goes about the business of managing the foreign affairs of a superpower in a dangerous and often hostile world, it is inevitable that the executive and legislative branches will disagree. When they do, how shall it be decided which is to prevail?

ROBERT A. GOLDWIN
ROBERT A. LICHT

1

Making Foreign Policy— The View from 1787

Jack N. Rakove

During the quarter-century separating the entrance of the United States into World War II from its intervention in Vietnam, American foreign policy commanded remarkably high support from both political parties and public opinion. The erosion of that consensus has led to renewed debate over the proper constitutional roles of the executive and legislative branches in the conduct of foreign relations. In the years since the adoption of the War Powers Act of 1973, the original criticism of an imperial presidency that had run amok in Indochina has been met by equally strong attacks on the dangers of allowing a meddlesome Congress to "micromanage" foreign policy. As is often the case in American politics, controversies about the wisdom of particular policies are cast in the language of constitutional principle. And since in practice Americans find it difficult to discuss the Constitution without appealing to its "original meaning," we again find ourselves discussing pressing issues from the vantage point of those eighteenth-century gentlemen who, for all their high hopes for the new republic, never anticipated the massive power the United States exerts in the contemporary world.

It would be easy to dismiss such appeals to the intentions of the framers as so much rhetoric designed to legitimate positions taken for other reasons. What are at stake, after all, are real and tough issues of current policy, not academic views of the ideas of 1787. Yet to the extent that disagreements about the proper roles of the executive and legislative branches are rooted in the text of the Constitution, reconstructing the concerns that led the framers to allocate the power over foreign affairs in the way they did may at least enable us to understand the sources of the jurisdictional difficulties that frequently bedevil the orderly conduct of American foreign policy.[1]

Foreign affairs loomed far larger in the movement that led to the writing of the Constitution than many scholars have been prepared to

1

recognize. True, a profound unease with the excesses of democratic misrule within the states explains why the framers came to Philadelphia convinced (as James Madison and Alexander Hamilton agreed) that their actions would "decide forever the fate of republican government."[2] But before 1787 it was the inability of the existing Continental Congress to frame and implement adequate foreign policies that evoked the most telling criticisms of the "imbecility" of the Articles of Confederation. Well into 1786 most efforts to amend the Articles were designed primarily to enable Congress to act effectively in the one area—the realm of foreign relations—where its responsibility was presumably least subject to question.

The essential foreign policy agenda of the newly independent republic emerged within a year of the conclusion of the Treaty of Paris, which recognized that the United States had indeed attained "among the powers of the earth, the separate and equal station" to which they were entitled by various authorities. Three issues posed serious challenges to the national welfare.[3]

First, Britain's refusal to open either the West Indies or the home islands to American shipping, coupled with the flooding of American markets with British ships carrying British goods, raised fundamental questions of commercial policy. The obvious strategy for the United States to pursue was to close its own harbors to British goods until Britain opened imperial ports to American ships. But since Congress had no authority to regulate either interstate or foreign commerce— unless it could conclude a treaty that Britain had no incentive to negotiate—retaliation required the adoption of identical restrictions by all the states. This proved impracticable.

A second issue arose from the refusal of particular states to comply with provisions of the peace treaty concerning the legal rights of private creditors, British subjects, and refugee loyalists who hoped to sue for the recovery of either prewar debts or confiscated property. Britain seized upon noncompliance with these articles as a pretext to retain control of its forts along the frontier—and thus to maintain its influence over hostile Indian nations in western New York and the lands above the Ohio River. This jeopardized congressional plans for settling the national domain, but again Congress could not compel the states to abide by the treaty.

Western expansion was also involved in the third major issue of postwar foreign policy, which stemmed from a Spanish decision of 1784 to close New Orleans and the lower Mississippi River to American navigation. A union that could not secure American access to the Gulf of Mexico might also lose the allegiance of the mass of settlers surging across the Appalachian chain from the east. Without independent sources of revenue, Congress lacked the means to project American power into the interior. But more than that, the sectional dimensions of the Mississippi question exposed the fragility of the American union, since southern leaders were far more committed to expansion into the Southwest than their counterparts in the North. The explosive potential of this became evident in 1786, when Secretary of Foreign Affairs John Jay (of New York) proposed that Congress abjure its claim to the Mississippi navigation in order to secure the commercial treaty he was then seeking to negotiate with Spain. Jay's request provoked a sharply sectional conflict within Congress, fueling speculation that the union might soon devolve into two or three regional confederacies.

The most striking aspect of these three issues is that they trenched far more deeply on problems of federalism than on the issues of separation of powers that so agitate us today. This was especially the case in the areas of commercial policy and treaty compliance, since both instances exposed the essential weakness of Congress vis-à-vis the states. Jay's request for a revision of his instructions raised a federal issue of a different but equally fundamental kind. By illuminating the widely divergent notions of sectional interest to which individual delegations in Congress had to be responsive, the furor over the Mississippi illustrated the tenuous character of the American union. It was an open question whether Americans could indeed recognize a transcendent national interest that would embody more than the sum or even a plurality of provincial or regional concerns.

Yet the foreign policy issues of the mid-1780s were not wholly devoid of implications for the Americans' evolving ideas about the separation of powers. The task of making the peace treaty binding on the states led naturally to consideration of the obligation of state judges to enforce federal acts over the conflicting laws of their own legislatures. That was exactly what James Duane sought to do in deciding *Rutgers* v. *Waddington* (1784), the celebrated case that is generally regarded as the first notable exercise of the power of judicial review.[4] But what if other state judges failed to follow Duane's example? In the absence of an independent federal judiciary or a clearer basis for elevating national acts above state law than Article XIII of the confederation could offer, the treaty issue remained a federal problem.

Arguably, Secretary Jay's dealings with Congress in 1786 also prefigured the efforts of the Federal Convention to divide power over foreign affairs between executive and legislative branches of government. In the midst of difficult negotiations with the Spanish emissary,

3

Jay felt bound to ask his superiors for new instructions. But instead of receiving a prompt response, he found that his request had only launched a protracted and bitter debate within Congress. The result, in all likelihood, left him unsurprised. For this was not the first time that a major debate over foreign policy had left Congress divided and paralyzed: seven years earlier Jay had played a central role in the equally bitter and more protracted debate that had erupted when the French minister to the United States asked Congress to define its prospective terms of peace.[5]

Clearly this was no way to manage delicate relations with the great powers of Europe. By the summer of 1786 experience had led Jay to "become daily more convinced," as he wrote Thomas Jefferson, "that the construction of our federal government is fundamentally wrong. To vest legislative, executive, and judicial powers in one and the same body of men, and that too in a body daily changing its members, can never be wise."[6] But Jay may have been peculiarly disposed to convert the frustrations of his own office into a recognition of the disadvantages of allowing a body like Congress to supervise the management of foreign relations so closely. Had he attended the Federal Convention, he might well have stated the case for a vigorous executive role in foreign affairs more effectively than anyone present managed to do. But Jay, alas, was not a delegate—and his absence has perhaps made our task of reconstructing the original intentions of the framers in the vital area of foreign affairs more difficult.

The Senate and Foreign Relations

However quaint this prior history of American foreign policy in the mid-1780s may seem today, a historian must insist that it is highly pertinent in at least one sense: it reminds us that the concerns of the framers were not the same as our own and that we cannot accordingly expect them to have given ample thought to the questions that perplex us today. They are not to be blamed for worrying more about state interference with national foreign policy than the potential evils of unratified executive agreements with other governments or the notification and withdrawal requirements of the War Powers Act.

With this admonition safely delivered, we can consider why the framers finally divided the power over foreign affairs in the way they did.

Many contemporary interpreters of the Constitution regard the placement of the treaty and appointment clauses within Article II (the executive article) as the best evidence that the framers intended to give the president the clear initiative and major role in the making of foreign policy and the conduct of foreign relations.[7] But from the vantage point of the historian, the great puzzle in tracing the convention's deliberations about the control of foreign relations is to explain why the president was given any significant authority at all. The central fact is that the two provisions on which claims for intended executive initiative in foreign affairs rest most explicitly—the power to make treaties and to appoint ambassadors—were adopted quite late in the convention and with remarkably little debate about their implications for the balance of authority between the executive and Congress. Well into August 1787 the framers appear to have assumed that the Senate would exercise the major responsibility for managing the nation's foreign relations.

It is easier to identify the assumptions on which the delegates first examined this issue than the concerns that led to their final decisions. For when the question of executive power was first taken up on June 1, James Wilson and James Madison both defined its scope in a way that made it clear that it did not extend to matters of "war and peace." The crucial point Wilson sought to establish was that "the prerogatives of the British Monarch" did not provide "a proper guide in defining the Executive powers. Some of these prerogatives were of a legislative nature. Among others [that is, among these] that of war & peace &c." Madison agreed that "executive powers ex vi termini, do not include the Rights of war & peace."[8]

These declarations reflected something more than a reflexive attempt to slay the bugbear of monarchicalism. Wilson and Madison were intent on having executive power "confined and defined" in a way that would distinguish it from the broader prerogative powers that the British crown exercised as a matter of historical right rather than of sound constitutional principle. The distinction was needed because British practice could otherwise be invoked to suggest that the powers to decide questions of war and peace or to make treaties or appoint ambassadors were inherently executive. Nor was this equation between executive power and power over foreign affairs derived from the British constitution alone. Because the Continental Congress held many of the powers formerly exercised by the crown—most notably in the realm of foreign affairs and war—some American commentators had treated this anomalous institution as being itself an executive body, notwithstanding its legislative features. At various times Congress had been described as "a deliberating executive assembly," "the supreme executive," or the "supreme executive council."[9] And in August 1785 Madison had noted (while discussing the state constitutions) "that all the great powers which are properly executive [had been] transferred to the federal government."[10] Charles Pinckney expressed the same idea when he opened the debate of June 1 by challenging that part of the Virginia plan that called for vesting the new executive with the executive powers of the existing Congress. These "might extend to war & peace," Pinckney warned, "which would render the executive a monarchy of the worst kind, to wit, an elective one."[11]

The key point, of course, is that this was exactly the point of confusion or uncertainty that Wilson and Madison succeeded in dispelling—as the absence of any countervailing opinions during the debate of June 1 suggests. If substantial powers over foreign affairs were to be lodged in the executive, it would require a positive decision of the convention, not an unthinking adaptation from British practice.

Nearly three months passed, however, before the delegates gave any further thought to the management of foreign relations. Much of the delay stemmed from the prolonged struggle over representation in the Senate and, once that was resolved, to the impasse over the mode of electing the president. Although these issues involved the two branches of government that would eventually share the treaty and appointive powers, nothing of note was said about the substantive duties each would exercise in those areas. Throughout this period the delegates apparently presumed that the Senate would play the dominant role in foreign relations. Thus when the Committee of Detail reported its draft constitution on August 6, the power "to make treaties, and to appoint ambassadors" was given exclusively to the Senate; the power to regulate foreign commerce was vested in Congress; and the executive was left with the heady function of receiving ambassadors—presumably when everyone else was out of town.[12]

Why was the Senate originally seen as the principal repository of authority over foreign affairs? The lack of any discussion of this issue before late August makes any answer to this question a matter of speculation, but several considerations probably conspired to favor the cause of the Senate—at least as long as the delegates were not prepared to examine the issue too closely or critically.

One consideration was probably the evident defects of the other branches of government. It is easy to understand how the prevailing imagery of the two chambers worked to favor the Senate against the House of Representatives. An upper chamber composed of a small, select group of experienced leaders who could debate crucial questions of policy in a considered manner appeared more trustworthy than a body of popularly elected legislators, less knowledgeable, serving shorter terms, and prey to the supposed passions that could infect large assemblies.

Beyond such considerations of institutional competence lay a broader set of assumptions about the nature of the new republic's international interests. When it came to imagining the kinds of relations the United States would have with other nations, it was far from clear how critical the proverbial executive virtues of secrecy, energy, and dispatch would prove in the successful management of foreign relations. One common idea of the 1780s was that relations with Europe would be governed by a small number of commercial treaties that should be negotiated with great care and that would thereafter provide a stable and pacific framework within which the nation could prosper in happy isolation from the vicissitudes of power politics. It was hoped that these treaties could be negotiated not by sending emissaries to foreign courts where they might be exposed to all manner of seductive temptations but rather by inviting foreign ministers to America. In this way it was possible to imagine that the Senate, after appointing a minister to serve as its agent, could in fact function as a direct party to negotiations.

Not everyone shared these optimistic assumptions about the brave new world of republican diplomacy, and indeed no informed leader could ignore the dangers that European colonial empires in North America still posed to American interests. But, again, the country's ability to withstand the destabilizing influence of the British to the north or of the Spanish to the southwest seemed to depend more on the essential reinvigoration of the union than on any particular arrangement of institutional power within the government. Moreover, insofar as the cohesion of the union required assuring different states and regions that their particular interests would be treated properly, there were advantages in vesting substantial foreign policy powers in a representative body like the Senate or even (in the case of the commerce power) the entire Congress. The president could finally come from only one state or region. But every state and region could be assured of having its voice heard in the Senate or Congress. For all its faults, the existing Congress had often functioned in this way, refusing to act on critical issues until it reached substantial agreement or even consensus. Delay, however aggravating, might sometimes be the price of decision.[13]

Yet if these considerations help to suggest why the Senate was originally regarded as the major player in foreign policy, in the end the problem is to explain why the convention belatedly chose to divide the treaty-making and appointive powers between the upper chamber and the president. Without abandoning their expectation that crucial decisions would be taken by the Senate, the delegates moved to enlarge the presidential role in the direction and implementation of foreign policy. Yet the fact that this shift did not evoke any extended discussion of the positive benefits of an expanded presidential role suggests that the final decisions on the foreign affairs powers constituted modest revisions rather than radical reappraisals.[14]

Perhaps the best place to begin considering why executive authority was enlarged is to ask what drawbacks the delegates might have perceived in allowing the Senate to remain the sole locus of authority in foreign affairs. The most obvious defect of the Senate lay in its disturbing resemblance to the existing Congress. Far from accepting the so-called Great Compromise of July 16 as an equitable balancing of the interests of large and small states, such delegates as Madison, Wilson, and Gouverneur Morris regarded the decision to give each state an equal vote in the Senate as a fundamental injustice that would preserve what Rufus King had denounced as "a vicious principle of representation."[15] They were equally alarmed by the consequences of allowing the state legislatures to elect the members of the upper house. For even if senators serving an extended term without the threat of recall would prove more independent of the state assemblies than delegates to Congress had been, they might still understandably choose to defer to the parochial desires of their constituents. Taken together, these two decisions undercut the expectations that had led Madison and his allies to hope that the Senate would emerge as the great fulcrum of the new regime.

These concerns help to explain why the delegates reacted so critically when the treaty clause was at last taken up on August 23.[16] The debate opened with Madison observing "that the Senate represented the States alone, and that for this as well as other obvious reasons it was proper that the President should be an agent in Treaties." But the ensuing discussion turned entirely away from the unspecified benefits of executive involvement to focus instead on the defects of the Senate. For in the remarks immediately following Madison's, Morris suggested that "he did not know that he should agree to refer the making of Treaties to the Senate at all" and then went on to move that "no Treaty shall be binding on the U.S. which is not ratified by a law." The intended effect of this amendment would be to introduce the House into the treaty process as a check on the Senate.

None of the delegates who responded to Morris's proposal revived Madison's earlier alternative suggestion of an executive role. Rather they discussed the Morris amendment on its merits. Nathaniel Gorham and William Samuel Johnson opposed it on the grounds that "there was something of a solecism in saying that the acts of a Minister with plenipotentiary powers from one Body, should depend for ratification on another Body." Wilson supported his colleague Morris's proposal because it provided a valuable check on the danger of the Senate's abusing its power. And in a brief but revealing comment John Dickinson of Delaware—a persistent advocate of conciliation between large and small states—endorsed the amendment "as most safe and proper, tho' he was sensible it was unfavorable to the little States; which would otherwise have an *equal* share in making Treaties."

Although the convention then roundly rejected Morris's amendment, eight states to one (Pennsylvania), with one state divided, it was apparent that the treaty clause was in trouble on several counts. As Edmund Randolph noted, "almost every speaker had made objections to the clause as it stood." Taken as a whole, Madison's notes of debate for August 23 reveal that the questions raised about allowing the Senate to control foreign relations reflected concern with both its representative character and the absence of any check on its actions. Only Madison, however, was prepared to look to the executive branch to remedy the defects of the Senate. At the very close of debate Madison again "hinted for consideration, whether a distinction might not be made between different sorts of Treaties—Allowing the President & Senate to make Treaties eventual and of Alliance for limited terms—and requiring the concurrence of the whole Legislature in other Treaties." Yet even Madison appears to have imagined only that the president would serve as the "agent" of the Senate while providing the same check that ratification by the House could afford on other occasions.

In its final action of August 23, the convention sent the entire treaty clause to the Committee of Detail. A week later that charge was superseded by a resolution establishing a new committee of one member from each state to consider "such parts of the Constitution as have been postponed, and such Reports as have not been acted upon." Significantly, its mandate thus included solving the vexing issue of presidential election. Among its members were Madison, Morris, King, Dickinson, and Roger Sherman.[17]

The President's Role in Foreign Affairs

It was in the lengthy second report of this committee, delivered on September 4, that the key alterations concerning both the treaty power and the executive nomination of ambassadors were made. Although Madison unfortunately left no record of its deliberations, there is good evidence that the committee engaged in a candid and wide-ranging debate about the proper allocation of the treaty power. In January 1788, when the South Carolina assembly was debating whether to call a ratification convention, Pierce Butler (a member of the committee) and General Charles C. Pinckney were asked to explain why the Philadelphia convention had joined the president and Senate in the treaty power. Their answers reveal that the committee had considered the cases to be made in favor of vesting power over foreign affairs in either the Senate or the House or Congress or the president. More than that, a few members of the committee did argue that the treaty power "might safely be lodged" in the executive alone. That smacked too much of monarchy to be acceptable, Butler noted. "The different propositions made on this subject occasioned much debate" within the committee, Pinckney added. "At last it was agreed to give the President a power of proposing treaties, as he was the ostensible head of the Union, and to vest the Senate (where each state had an equal voice) with the power of agreeing or disagreeing to the terms proposed."[18]

Here at last is evidence that some of the framers were envisioning an executive who could act in foreign affairs as more than either an agent of the Senate or a check on it. Even if the recollections of the South Carolina delegates do not fully recount the reasoning that prevailed in the committee, they at least indicate that its decision to place the treaty clause in the executive article was not just a quirk of draftsmanship. And this inference is further supported by the committee's concurrent effort to solve the thorny issue of presidential election.

The revised version of the treaty clause was the seventh of the nine items that the committee presented in its report of September 4. The same report contained the committee's proposal for the electoral college, and it was this topic that preoccupied the delegates for three days before they turned to the treaty clause on September 7. Although during the debate on the electoral college the treaty power was mentioned only in passing, the final decisions on presidential election provide a critical link in understanding why the convention then went on to accept a major presidential role in treaty making.

The controversial feature of the electoral college lay in the committee's proposal that the Senate should make the final selection whenever the electors failed to produce a majority for any candidate—as many delegates expected would usually be the case. As Randolph, George Mason, Wilson, John Rutledge, and Charles Pinckney all made clear, this would create "such an influence in the Senate over the election of the President in addition to its other powers, [as] to convert that body into a real and dangerous Aristocracy." Morris responded that the Senate was now less dangerous than it had been before the committee had divided its powers over treaties and appointments with the executive. But as Hugh Williamson (another committee member) replied, "The aristocratic complexion proceeds from the change in the mode of appointing the President which makes him dependent on the Senate."[19]

The delegates stumbled onto the solution to this problem almost literally as an afterthought. Transferring the power of contingent election from the Senate to the House (voting by states) preserved the ostensible compromise between small and large states while "lessening the influence of the Senate" over the president.[20] The net effect of this decision was to enhance the authority of the president over and against that of the Senate. With this vote the executive had ceased to be politically dependent on the body with which it would share the power over treaties and appointments once the other part of the committee's report (relating to foreign affairs) was adopted.

The likelihood that reservations about the Senate had already led the delegates to accept an enlarged executive role in foreign affairs is further supported by the tenor of the actual discussion of the treaty clause on September 7 and 8. What seems most remarkable is how little the delegates had to say about the presidential role. After rebutting a final effort by the Pennsylvania delegation to include the House of Representatives in treaty making, the convention quickly approved the first part of the treaty clause as it now stands. No one objected to the reformulation stating that the "President by and with the advice and consent of the Senate, shall have power to make treaties."[21]

What *was* controversial was the committee's further proposal requiring a two-thirds vote of the Senate for the approval of treaties. It was in the context of the reasonableness of this requirement, rather than the vesting of the treaty power in the president and Senate per se, that the delegates touched on the role they expected the executive to play. The challenge to the two-thirds rule ran along two complementary lines. First, large state delegates objected to it because it would enable a minority of states—and in theory a disproportionately smaller minority of the population—"to controul the will of a majority." On this point, as King noted, the "check" of a supermajority was unnecessary because "the Executive was here joined in the business."[22]

The second challenge apparently arose from a concern of particular importance to Madison, who pursued a rather complex parliamentary strategy. Madison first secured unanimous approval for an amendment exempting treaties of peace from the two-thirds requirement, on the grounds that these should "be made with less difficulty than other treaties." But he then moved to restore the two-thirds rule for peace treaties while eliminating "the concurrence of the Presi-

11

dent," on the grounds that the executive "would necessarily derive so much importance from a state of war that he might be tempted, if authorized, to impede a treaty of peace." This motion elicited two notable comments. Butler seconded the proposal "as a necessary security against ambitious & corrupt Presidents." More intriguing was the opposing view of Morris, who argued "that no peace ought to be made without the concurrence of the President, who was the general Guardian of the National interests." The convention's rejection of this amendment (eight states to three) suggests that many delegates found Morris's image of a patriot president more appealing than Butler's fears of potential presidential perfidy. Given the opportunity to exclude the president from a vital diplomatic duty, the delegates explicitly voted for executive involvement.[23]

With this amendment safely dispatched, the convention returned to the issue of the two-thirds rule on September 8. In a final flurry of motions, it rejected Madison's first amendment (eliminating the two-thirds rule for peace treaties), a final effort by Wilson to have all treaties made by simple majorities, and four additional attempts to enlarge the senatorial quorum (and thus make the two-thirds barrier even higher). In its final vote on the treaty power, the convention endorsed the provision as if it had come from the committee on postponed parts.[24]

What sense can we make of the convention's deliberations on the treaty clause? Clearly the delegates had come to perceive the benefits of both presidential involvement and independence in the negotiation of treaties. But did their acceptance of these ideas amount as well to an endorsement of presidential initiative in the making of foreign policy and a corresponding reduction of the senatorial duty of advice and consent to mere ratification of the acts of a superior executive?

Any definitive answer to this question is precluded by the fact that the delegates had so little to say about the role they expected the president to play in the overall conduct of foreign policy. One could, of course, interpret the delegates' failure to discuss this very question more seriously as evidence that they had already consciously accepted a radical shift in the locus of decision making from the Senate to the president. Such a reading, though plausible in theory, is far from persuasive. Given the animus against executive power that had been expressed in the original debate of June 1, it seems highly unlikely that so crucial a change could have been made without generating a debate far more extensive and heated than the one that actually took place. The almost incidental way in which the delegates discussed the new executive involvement in treaty making suggests rather that they interpreted the changes proposed by the committee on postponed parts in much more modest terms. By contrast, the final efforts to tinker with the nuances of the two-thirds proviso indicate that many delegates were convinced that the Senate would remain the crucial forum of decision. Moreover, there is little basis for concluding that the framers thought of the senatorial duty of "advice and consent" as merely a post hoc review of diplomatic initiatives undertaken independently by the president. The fear that the particular interests of individual states might be materially harmed by treaties naturally led the delegates to expect that the representatives of the states would have to enjoy a say in drafting the instructions under which ambassadors were to operate.

On balance, the belated revisions that laid the strongest foundation for a major executive role in foreign policy are more safely explained as a cautious reaction against the defects of exclusive senatorial control of foreign relations than as a bold attempt to convert the novel office of a republican presidency into a vigorous national leader in world affairs. At the minimum, the idea that the president could serve as the "agent" of the Senate may have reflected an appreciation of the administrative awkwardness and redundancy that would arise if the executive were entirely excluded from the enterprise of treaty making. Assuming that a department of foreign affairs would be necessary to manage routine diplomatic and consular business, the principle of a unitary executive would be violated if the Senate were allowed to maintain its own independent diplomatic channels.[25] Probably more important, however, were the reservations about the Senate that several key proponents of presidential involvement—Madison, Wilson, and Morris—all expressed. Had the Senate been constructed along the lines they originally favored, they might well have been content to allow the president to do nothing more notable in the realm of foreign relations than conduct routine correspondence, receive ambassadors, and carry on such further tasks as the Senate (or Congress) in its wisdom saw fit to delegate.

The Framers' Intentions

Yet if these are the most prudent conclusions that can be drawn about the framers' intentions on the basis of the debates of 1787, one cannot rule out the possibility that at least some of them hoped to lay a foundation that would enable and even encourage the president to act, in Morris's words, "as the general Guardian of the National interests." Certainly their own experience could have led them to appreciate the potential benefits of giving the president some leeway to control the process of diplomacy. This would be especially the case

13

if active presidential supervision of negotiations worked to deter or reduce the kinds of political conflict that had erupted in 1779 and 1786, when the Continental Congress found itself mired in bitter dispute over major issues of foreign policy. Without denying either the right of the Senate to offer its advice in advance of actual negotiations or the obligation of the president to seek it, the delegates could envision situations in which a president who enjoyed the confidence of the Senate might exercise substantial initiative. More than that, the advice of the Senate would amount to something less than instructions in the strict sense of the term. As Wilson reminded the Pennsylvania ratifying convention in early December 1787, the Senate could not force the president to make a treaty he did not approve.[26]

In this sense, then, the decisions of September 1787 clearly made the president into something more than the mere agent of the Senate—but also rather less than an American version of the British Crown. And that was how the relevant clauses of the Constitution were perceived during the ratification debates that followed. The first commentators on the Constitution did not suppose that the convention had created an overmighty executive whose rash actions would imperil the security of the nation. Critics of the treaty clause did not argue that it would enable the president to exercise an independent, much less decisive, role in the conduct of foreign relations. Anti-Federalist objections instead rested on a dual fear: either that an aristocratic Senate would dominate the president or that the array of sordid motives that eighteenth-century Americans attributed to all officeholders would lead the two branches to collude in sacrificing the national good. The perceived danger lay in joint presidential-senatorial misconduct so guilefully contrived that even the two-thirds proviso would prove inadequate. Suppose, for example, that the president, conspiring with senators from one section of the country, secretly negotiated a treaty and then suddenly summoned the Senate into session. Seven states could make a quorum; two-thirds of a quorum could ratify a treaty; ergo, ten senators from five states could transmute a treacherous negotiation into a treaty binding as the supreme law of the land.[27]

On the other side of the question, supporters of the Constitution defended the treaty clause as a prudent allocation of authority between two equal branches. The most notable explications of the treaty power appear in essays 64 and 75 of *The Federalist*, written respectively by Jay, secretary of foreign affairs, and Hamilton. Jay stressed the advantages of "perfect *secrecy* and immediate *despatch*" that the president would bring to negotiation. But it is equally clear that he expected the Senate to play the leading role in deciding what policies the president would pursue. "Those matters which in negotiations usually require the most secrecy and the most despatch," Jay wrote, "are those preparatory and auxiliary measures which are not otherwise important in a national view, than as they tend to facilitate the attainment of the objects of the negotiation." It was in the determination of those objects that the "talents, information, integrity, and deliberate investigations" of the Senate would prove most useful. Nothing in the experienced Jay's treatment of this issue equates the pragmatic advantages of executive expeditiousness with the right to initiate or set policy. "Should any circumstance occur which requires the advice and consent of the Senate," he observed, the president "may at any time convene them."[28]

Hamilton's discussion of the treaty power is especially interesting because it expresses ideas rather different from the positions he would take in the early 1790s, when his defense of broad executive authority in foreign affairs played a critical role in crystallizing the party conflicts between Federalists and Republicans. *Federalist* No. 75 is noteworthy in two respects. First, against the argument that the power to make treaties belonged "in the class of executive authorities," Hamilton responded that treaty making was "a distinct department" of government that properly belonged to neither legislature nor executive alone but could reasonably be divided between them. Alluding to Jay's earlier essay, Hamilton noted that the distinctive qualities of executive efficiency made the president "the most fit agent" for conducting negotiations, "while the vast importance of the trust, and the operation of treaties as laws, plead strongly for the participation of the whole or a portion of the legislative body in the office of making them."[29]

Second, and somewhat more striking, Hamilton found it more difficult to justify any presidential involvement in treaty making than to explain why the power could not have been entrusted to the Senate alone. Echoing Butler, Hamilton observed that ambition and avarice might easily tempt the president to "betray the interests of the state. . . . The history of human conduct," he added,

> does not warrant the exalted opinion of human virtue which would make it wise to commit interests of so delicate and momentous a kind, as those which concern its intercourse with the rest of the world, to the sole disposal of a magistrate created and circumstanced as would be a President of the United States.

In theory the Senate could have been left free to decide whether or when to employ the president as its diplomatic agent. But this seemed

15

unwise for two reasons. First, the president, as "the constitutional representative of the nation," would enjoy greater "confidence and respect" than would the mere "ministerial representative of the Senate." Second, "his participation would materially add to the safety of the society" by providing an effective check against the abuse of senatorial power.

Elsewhere in the debates over ratification one occasionally encounters more expansive descriptions of the presidential role in the conduct of negotiations.[30] Yet on balance there is little evidence that the ratifiers expected either that the president would have the dominant voice in the making of foreign policy or that the Senate would be reduced to acting as a mere check on the executive. Such possibilities may have been latent in the text of the Constitution, notably in the placement of the treaty and appointive powers within Article II and, perhaps more significantly, in the institutional advantages that the executive could derive from its management of routine business with foreign nations. But, taken as a whole, the records of 1787–1788 do not sustain the broad notions of plenary presidential power that have again been voiced as part of the current reaction against the dangers of excessive congressional meddling in foreign relations.

The expectation of shared power, the idea that the president was as much a check on the Senate as vice versa, and the substantial powers over foreign relations vested in Congress in Article I, all create awkward obstacles for those who want to legitimate the subsequent evolution of executive power over foreign affairs with the language of original intent. This is especially the case if one accepts the strict criterion of "originalism" that holds that only those interpretations of the Constitution that were publicly articulated and accepted at the moment of its adoption can be regarded as authoritative (because they alone entered into the process of ratification that gave the Constitution its juridical status as supreme law). As Madison would repeatedly argue, the expansive notions of executive power that Hamilton and his allies espoused after 1789—smacking as they did of monarchical prerogative—would probably have doomed the Constitution to rejection had they been advanced in 1787–1788 and were for that very reason illegitimate and incorrect.

Yet neither can one ignore the obvious consequences that flowed simply from the creation of a unitary presidency charged with the oversight of the subordinate departments of the executive branch. From the start it seems likely that at least some of the framers and ratifiers of 1787–1788 privately glimpsed the potential openings for executive initiativethat lay implicit in the spare language of the constitutional text—and that successive administrations, beginning with

George Washington's, soon began to exploit. As Publius, Jay could plausibly argue that presidential discretion in foreign affairs would be confined to those "preparatory and auxiliary measures which . . . tend to facilitate the attainment of the objects of the negotiation," but his own experience had certainly taught him just how much leeway a diplomat could exercise once negotiations in a distant place were under way. In 1782, after all, Jay had taken the lead in persuading his colleagues on the American peace commission to ignore their instructions from Congress and not keep their French allies informed of the terms of their bilateral negotiations with Britain. Nor does it strain credibility to suggest that the balanced analysis of the treaty clause in *Federalist* No. 75 did not fully or accurately reflect Hamilton's own reading of the possibilities latent in the constitutional text. By 1793 (if not earlier) he was prepared to argue that the specific powers relating to foreign affairs that the Constitution had delegated to either the Senate or Congress were to be regarded as explicit exceptions to a general and inherent executive authority to manage foreign relations.

Hamilton's elaboration of this doctrine in his Pacificus letters of 1793 led a reluctant Madison, at the urging of Secretary of State Jefferson, to take up his pen (as Helvidius) in rebuttal. At issue was the response of the United States to the outbreak of war between Britain and revolutionary France. The central question was whether it had been within the legitimate power of President Washington to issue a unilateral proclamation declaring that the United States would act impartially toward the belligerents, without first requesting the advice of the Senate (or Congress) to determine what obligations the nation had toward France under the treaty of alliance of 1778. The nuances of the arguments deployed matter less than the fact of the debate itself, which is noteworthy in two vital respects.

The first and most obvious point to be made, of course, is that disputes over the scope of the foreign policy powers of the executive and legislative branches are virtually coeval with the Republic. The early (not to say immediate) emergence of the divergent positions that we associate with Hamilton and Madison seems to suggest that there is something illusory (or delusory) about attempting to recover some pristine, unsullied original meaning of the relevant clauses of the Constitution. Perhaps the best one can do is to recover the range of considerations, not entirely consistent, that led the framers to vest substantial authority over foreign relations in the legislature while providing the president with a degree of independence that might, over time, evolve into a capacity for the initiation and direction of foreign policy. Much of our history since 1789 has, of course, demonstrated that the formal powers vested in Congress or the Senate alone can rarely match the institutional advantages that the executive enjoys.

Just how easily presidential independence could lead to initiative was one of the many lessons Madison had to absorb in the 1790s. For in the course of his efforts to check Hamilton's Anglophilic foreign policy, Madison was pained to discover how difficult it was to convert his understanding of the true meaning of the Constitution into an effective political result. Repeatedly in the mid-1790s he sought to mobilize "the Republican interest" in Congress to counteract Federalist foreign policy. While recognizing that the executive branch, as a permanent government-in-being, would often have to respond to urgent developments, Madison appears to have supposed that the administration should temper its decisions so as not to prevent Congress from exercising its right to have an active voice in formulating foreign policy. But experience quickly taught him that Congress was an unwieldy instrument. It proved difficult not only to muster any kind of consensus among his colleagues—especially when that meant opposing President Washington—but also to prevent the administration from using its control of vital information and the long recesses of Congress to structure the debate in its own favor and to sway public opinion. Repeated frustration led Madison to a bitter conclusion. "The management of foreign relations," he wrote Jefferson in May 1798,

> appears to be the most susceptible of abuse of all the trusts committed to a Government, because they can be concealed or disclosed, or disclosed in such parts and at such times as will best suit particular views; and because the body of the people are less capable of judging, and are more under the influence of prejudices, on that branch of their affairs, than of any other.[31]

One need not wonder whether Hamilton was equally skeptical of the capacity of Congress to pursue sage and consistent foreign policies in a dangerous world.

Conclusion

The early emergence of these contending views of the roles of the executive and the legislature does not, however, entirely require us to follow E. S. Corwin's famous formulation and view the constitutional division of authority over foreign affairs as an invitation to the political branches to struggle for supremacy. The Constitution does not so much invite struggle as permit it to flourish once it has arisen for other reasons—reasons that are almost invariably rooted in different views of national interest rather than principled notions of how foreign policy should be made in the abstract. What first separated the Republicans and Federalists of the 1790s were substantive disagreements over whether American interests—economic, political, strategic, and even ideological—would be better served by "tilting" toward revolutionary France or monarchical Britain. If we could always agree where our true interests lie, the untidiness inherent in the Constitution would matter little. But for most of our history, consensus about foreign policy has proved far more elusive than most Americans, with their chronically stunted recall of the past, realize.

To say that constitutional arguments are often instrumental does not mean, of course, that they are always or merely instrumental. Nor does it mean that the contemporary debate about the proper conduct of foreign policy must always be constrained by partisan preferences. There are principled as well as expedient cases to be made for most of the claims and counterclaims that have animated the jurisdictional disputes of recent years. Defenders of executive initiative have good reason to ask whether congressional "micromanagement" of foreign policy is conducive to the protection of the national interest. Critics of presidential adventurism can similarly argue that any administration that proves incapable of mustering a congressional consensus in support of a particular policy would be well advised to recognize that discretion is indeed often the better part of valor.

Yet in practice the line between political concerns and constitutional principles is hard to draw and even more difficult to maintain. The very diversity and complexity of American economic interests in the world, the moralist strain of American foreign policy, the pace of political change among both our allies and our adversaries, all promise to make the task of defining the "true" national interest more difficult, not less, in the polycentric world that is now replacing the binary divisions of midcentury. So, too, the prospect that control of Congress and the executive may be indefinitely divided between the two parties almost guarantees that disagreements over policy will periodically escalate into disputes about the constitutional allocation of power. Whether or not such conflicts are consistent with the original intentions of the framers, they have certainly become part of what the Constitution means today.

2

Principle, Prudence, and the Constitutional Division of Foreign Policy

Nathan Tarcov

How should a government conceived in liberty and dedicated to the proposition that all men are created equal conduct its foreign policy? How should its institutions be constituted and operate for the purpose of conducting foreign policy? Such questions transcend historical or legal inquiry and compel us to reconsider the debates among the American founders, not to uncover some unequivocal and authoritative original intent, but to help us understand the fundamental problem underlying the founders' and our own struggles to answer these questions.

In considering how a government instituted to secure inalienable rights and deriving its just powers from the consent of the governed should conduct its foreign policy, a good place to begin is with the great philosopher John Locke. That Locke discussed such issues in the context of late seventeenth-century monarchical England rather than either in emphatically republican late eighteenth-century America or in decidedly democratic late twentieth-century America need not render his discussion less illuminating. On the contrary, it may help us to distinguish those aspects of our situation that result from our liberalism from those that relate specifically to our republicanism or democracy.

Locke's Foreign Affairs Power

Locke divides political power into three distinct areas. These are not, however, the executive, legislative, and judicial powers that are familiar to Americans; rather, they are the legislative, executive, and "federative" or foreign affairs power. Locke's way of dividing political power helps to clarify for us why the American founders and we as their heirs have difficulty fitting the conduct of foreign policy institutionally into a structure defined by legislative, executive, and judicial branches and theoretically into a polity inspired by the rule of law and conformity to moral principle.

Locke defines political power in the first chapter of the *Second Treatise* as follows:

> *Political Power* then I take to be *a Right* of making Laws with Penalties of Death, and consequently all less Penalties, for the Regulating and Preserving of Property, and of employing the force of the Community, in the Execution of such Laws, and in the defence of the Common-wealth from Foreign Injury, and all this only for the Publick Good.[1]

The division suggested by this definition, significantly for our purposes, at first appears twofold: making laws and exerting force—legislation and execution. The force of the community, however, is exerted in two very different ways—in executing the laws and in defending the community from foreign injury. These two powers have in common that they both employ the force of the community, but by making this distinction Locke indicates that the defense of the community from foreign injury cannot be conceived or conducted as if it were execution of laws made by the community.

When Locke first explains the origin of political power and defines political society, he emphasizes only the legislative and executive powers,[2] but that is only because only those powers distinguish those "who are, and who are not, in *Political Society* together." Having a commonly accepted legislative body and laws and an authorized agency for enforcing those laws distinguishes those who live in civil society from those who do not. Reliance upon force to defend against injury in the absence of accepted legislators, laws, and enforcers is common both to those who live in what Locke calls the state of nature and to those who live in a civil society insofar as they enter into relations with the rest of mankind.

Locke proceeds immediately, however, to emphasize instead the distinction between the legislative and foreign affairs powers. He says that

> the Commonwealth comes by a Power to set down, what punishment shall belong to the several transgressions which they think worthy of it, committed amongst the Members of that Society, (which is the *power of making Laws*) as well as it has the power to punish any Injury done unto any of its Members, by any one that is not of it, (which is the *power of War and Peace*).

Locke thereby presents both the legislative and the foreign affairs powers in legalistic terms insofar as both are described as involving punishment, but the power of war and peace does not seem to involve setting down the punishments in advance.[3]

Locke quickly clarifies that point by his definition of the

> *Executive Power* of Civil Society, which is to judge by standing Laws how far Offences are to be punished, when committed within the Commonwealth; and also to determin, by occasional Judgments founded on the present Circumstances of the Fact, how far Injuries from without are to be vindicated, and in both these to imploy all the force of all the Members when there shall be need.[4]

In determining how far to punish or vindicate both offenses committed within the commonwealth and injuries from without, the executive power exercises judgment—neither is a matter of nondiscretionary application. (In his chapter on prerogative, Locke argues that the executive should have, among other prerogative powers, "a Power, in many Cases, to mitigate the severity of the Law, and pardon some Offenders.")[5] The executive must judge how far to punish offenses committed within the commonwealth by standing laws made by the legislative, whereas it must determine how far to vindicate injuries from without by occasional judgments founded on the present circumstances of the fact. Not only are injuries from without condemned otherwise than as violations of standing laws, and their vindication measured otherwise than by punishments set down in advance, but force is to be used at least as much to prevent as to redress them in order to "secure the Community from Inroads and Invasion."[6]

The foreign affairs power for Locke differs fundamentally from the legislative and executive powers in that it may be called "*natural*, because it is that which answers to the Power every Man naturally had before he entered into Society."[7] In the state of nature, as Locke calls the condition of men when they have not entered into civil society with one another and established a common legislative and executive, individuals cannot make laws or therefore execute laws they have made to govern one another. The legislative and executive powers are artificial powers that exist only within civil society as a result of consent to create them.

Although the legislative and executive powers are absent in the state of nature, individuals in that condition do have two other powers, which correspond to the foreign affairs power in civil society. The first is the power to do whatever they think reasonable to preserve their own life, liberty, and property against the injuries and attempts of others, including the right to seek reparation for damage. The second is the power to judge and punish as they see fit violations of the law of nature so as to restrain, deter, and even—if they think it necessary—destroy transgressors and to preserve the rest of mankind.[8] In entering civil society, individuals surrender the first power only insofar as is required to preserve their own life, liberty, and property and those of the rest of society and therefore retain the residue, but they surrender the second power entirely.[9] These surrenders give rise to the legislative and executive as well as to the federative powers of civil government, but in the case of the legislative and executive powers the surrendered natural powers are transformed into new powers, whereas in the case of the foreign affairs power they are merely transferred to the community and its authorized agent.

The foreign affairs power might seem not to differ so radically from the legislative and executive powers that involve standing law because its corresponding natural powers also involve a law—that of nature. The first power of an individual in the state of nature is to do whatsoever he thinks fit for the preservation of himself and others "within the permission of the *Law of Nature*" and the second is to execute that law.[10]

The law of nature, however, differs in several important respects from civil law, and the foreign affairs power therefore remains radically different from the legislative and executive powers. For even though Locke asserts that the state of nature has a law of nature to govern it that obligates everyone, he explains that in that condition

> There wants an *establish'd*, settled, known *Law*, received and allowed by common consent to be the Standard of Right and Wrong, and the common measure to decide all Controversies between them. For though the Law of Nature be plain and intelligible to all rational Creatures; yet Men being biassed by their Interest, as well as ignorant for want of study of it, are not apt to allow of it as a Law binding to them in the application of it to their particular Cases.[11]

Similarly, Locke points out, the law of nature lacks a *"known and indifferent Judge"* with authority to determine differences according to it, leaving parties partial to themselves to be "both Judge and Executioner." Its would-be executors lack not only common acceptance and impartiality but all too often *"Power* to back and support the Sentence when right."[12] Thus despite the law of nature, the power of individuals in the state of nature and, by analogy, the foreign affairs power lack the commonly accepted rule and impartial and effective enforcement that mark the legislative and executive powers. Most important, the foreign affairs power may sometimes have the character of punishing or vindicating injuries under a law but it does so against parties who have not consented to that power.

Furthermore, the law of nature for Locke seems to be not a code prohibiting specific actions under pain of specific punishments in a manner parallel to civil law, but a broad command that serves as the standard both for civil law and for the foreign affairs power. The law of nature is simply another word for human reason, man's "only Star and compass."[13] Fundamentally what it teaches is the preservation of all mankind as much as possible.[14] To say that civil laws are "only so far right, as they are founded on the Law of Nature, by which they are to be regulated and interpreted" is to say fundamentally that they must be conformable to the preservation of mankind.[15] As Locke writes elsewhere, "the Preservation of all Mankind, as much as in him lies . . . is every one's Duty, and the true Principle to regulate our Religion, Politicks and Morality by."[16] Conformity to this broad principle leaves the foreign affairs power still a matter of occasional judgments founded on present circumstances rather than an "executive" power in relation to a natural legal code parallel to the executive power in relation to the civil legal code.

Locke explains that the foreign affairs power, which answers to the power every individual naturally had before entering into civil society, "contains the Power of War and Peace, Leagues and Alliances, and all the Transactions, with all Persons and Communities without the Commonwealth." Locke's suggested name of "*Federative*, if any one pleases" (although he remains "indifferent as to the Name") emphasizes leagues and alliances (and the keeping of faith that renders them binding on independent communities), but he is also willing to call it the power of war and peace. (He does not, however, necessarily include within it the British monarch's power to initiate or terminate war—the kings of the Indians in America command absolutely in war, "which admits not of Plurality of Governours," yet the resolutions of peace and war belong ordinarily to the people or a council.)[17] He immediately redescribes it as "the management of the *security and interest of the publick without*, with all those that it may receive benefit or damage from."[18] This redescription in itself brings out the distinctive character of the federative power: it involves management rather than execution; security and interest rather than law; benefit and damage rather than rights and injuries.

Locke follows this pregnant redescription of the foreign affairs power with his most important statement of the difference and even tension between that power and the legislative and executive powers:

it is much less capable to be directed by antecedent, standing, positive Laws, than the *Executive;* and so must necessarily be left to the Prudence and Wisdom of those whose
hands it is in, to be managed for the publick good. For the
Laws that concern Subjects one amongst another, being to
direct their actions, may well enough *precede* them. But what
is to be done in reference to *Foreigners,* depending much
upon their actions, and the variation of designs and interests, must be *left* in great part *to* the *Prudence* of those who
have this Power committed to them, to be managed by the
best of their Skill, for the advantage of the Commonwealth.[19]

The foreign affairs power is much less capable than the executive
power of being directed by laws because it is much less capable than
the legislative power of directing by laws those with whom it deals.
The legislative and executive powers direct the actions of subjects; the
foreign affairs power does not direct the actions of foreigners. It does
not have the power—power in the sense either of right or of force—to
direct the actions of foreigners and independent communities. They
have not consented to be so directed and they have the capability to
resist. The foreign affairs power must instead respond to the actions
and to reasonable estimates of the intentions and interests of foreigners.

Fitting this prudential power, which is neither lawmaking nor
law-enforcing, into a governmental structure of legislative and executive powers is necessarily problematic. Conceiving civil government as legislative and executive (including for now the judicial
within the executive in the Lockean fashion) seems to be a straightforward requirement of the liberal principle of rule of law. The primary
purpose of establishing civil government is to establish the rule of law,
to ensure that men are subject to no authority that does not act by
making or enforcing standing laws.[20] Owing to this primacy of the
rule of law, the legislative is for Locke the supreme power within a
constituted commonwealth (the people retain a residual supremacy).[21]

Locke justifies the supremacy of the legislative power as follows:

For what can give Laws to another, must needs be superiour
to him: and since the Legislative is no otherwise Legislative
of the Society, but by the right it has to make Laws for all the
parts and for every Member of the Society, prescribing Rules
to their actions, and giving power of Execution, where they
are transgressed, the *Legislative* must needs be the *Supream,*
and all other Powers in any Members or parts of the Society,
derived from and subordinate to it.[22]

This justification of legislative supremacy appears to presume the possibility of the legislative power's prescribing rules for all other powers, although it makes no explicit reference to the federative power that is quite incapable of being so directed.

Legislative supremacy over the foreign affairs power is made explicit shortly thereafter:

> When the *Legislative* hath put the *Execution* of the Laws, they make, into other hands, they have a power still to resume it out of those hands, when they find cause, and to punish for any mall-administration against the Laws. The same holds also in regard of the *Federative* Power, that and the Executive being both *Ministerial and subordinate to the Legislative*, which as has been shew'd in a Constituted Commonwealth, is the Supream.[23]

Neither the general justification of legislative supremacy nor this specific application of legislative impeachment to the foreign affairs power takes account, however, of the difficulty of directing the foreign affairs power by standing laws and the consequent need to leave it to the prudence of those who manage it. The legislative power to resume the executive power and to punish for maladministration against the laws is said to apply also to the foreign affairs power, although that power is not one of executing laws made by the legislative. The foreign affairs power is said to be ministerial to the legislative like the executive even though it cannot be directed by lawmaking.

From the perspective of legislative supremacy, the problem seems to be how to keep the federative power subordinate given the difficulty of directing it by standing laws. From the perspective of prudent foreign policy, the problem seems to be how to leave its conduct free from direction by standing laws given its subordination to the legislative. If foreign affairs cannot be directed effectively by standing laws but every power is subordinate to the legislative, then the practical alternatives are that the foreign affairs power is poorly directed by inappropriate standing laws, that the legislative power and the law lose their supremacy, that the legislative find ways to subordinate the foreign affairs power other than by directing its operations through laws (impeachment, investigation, etc.), or some combination of those alternatives.

Locke's insistence on the rule of law might seem undefeated by the need for prudent foreign policy since the rule of law is meant to apply to subjects of the commonwealth, not foreigners. A foreign affairs power that is not directed by standing laws, however, uses the force of subjects in its operations and even requires their absolute obedience as soldiers.[24] In addition, the difficulty of subordinating the foreign affairs power to the legislative may affect the subordination of the executive as well. For the executive and federative powers are "hardly to be separated" since they both require the force of the society for their exercise and it is "almost impracticable to place the Force of the Commonwealth in distinct, and not subordinate hands."[25] A united executive-federative power that cannot be directed by standing laws in its federative operations may well, therefore, prove resistant to subordination to the legislative in its domestic operations as well.

These problems are mitigated in theory but exacerbated in practice by the fact that Locke's doctrine of legislative supremacy requires only subordinating the executive power as such to the legislative power as such, but not subordinating an executive who shares in the legislative power (such as the English king or the American president) to the rest of the legislative.[26] This distinction prevents a theoretical contradiction between legislative supremacy and an independent executive, but it complicates the practical problem of legislative control over foreign affairs. Executive participation in the legislative power opens the possibility of subordinating the foreign affairs power to laws passed with the consent of the executive-federative branch— laws that may still be inappropriately general and inflexible (that is to say lawlike), not to mention laws passed over the constitutional objection of the executive-federative branch. Executive participation in the legislative power may also serve as a counterpoise in an uneasy balance with the efforts of the legislative branch to control the foreign affairs power through laws and other means.

The problem of fitting the foreign affairs power into a governmental structure of legislative and executive powers is not simply that conducting foreign affairs differs from both making law and executing law. If conducting foreign affairs were entirely a matter of prudence without any quasi-legal component of conformity to general principle, then it would seem simply disjoined from the legislative power while necessarily adhering to the executive in a manner that removes the executive from neat subordination to the legislative. Subordination to the legislative would then seem to be only an attempt at approximating the rule of law rather than an expression of any inherent aspect of the foreign affairs power itself. The foreign affairs power, as we have seen, operates by occasional judgments founded on present circumstances; it greatly depends on the actions and the varying intentions and interests of foreigners; and, consequently, it must necessarily be left in great part to the prudence of those to whom it is committed. It still must try, however, to conform to the broad principles of natural law, to such general dictates of our reason as that all mankind should be preserved as much as possible, that compacts should be regarded as binding, that other peoples should not be governed without their consent, and that reparations for war damages may be claimed from aggressors but not from the innocent and not to the extent of territorial annexation.[27] The conduct of foreign affairs involves both prudential and quasi-legal components.

The duality between principle and prudence within Locke's foreign affairs power reflects a broader duality within his conception of politics. He writes elsewhere that "Politics contains two parts very different the one from the other, the one containing the original of societies and the rise and extent of political power, the other, the art of governing men in society."[28] He recommends there the anonymous *Two Treatises* for the first part and experience and history for learning the art of government. He also calls the first the general part of civil law, which teaches "the natural Rights of Men, and the Original and Foundations of Society, and the Duties resulting from thence" and concerns "the Affairs and Intercourse of civilized Nations in general, grounded upon Principles of Reason."[29]

The duality within the Lockean or liberal foreign affairs power between conformity to general principle and prudent management for the public interest is expressed institutionally by the dual imperatives of subordination to the legislative power and incapability of being directed by standing laws. Subordination to the legislative power corresponds to the quasi-legal component of the foreign affairs power; its conformity to general principle. Incapability of being directed by standing laws corresponds to its prudential component, its dependence on varying circumstances, and uncontrollable foreign actions, intentions, and interests.

Neither component of the foreign affairs power should blind us to the other or to its institutional expression. To say that foreign policy should conform to principle is not to rule out prudence. The principles in question are broad ones that leave plenty of room for prudence. The obligations of Lockean natural law are far from incompatible with skillful management of the national security and national interest. After all, "the *first and fundamental natural Law,* which is to govern even the Legislative it self, is *the preservation of the Society,* and (as far as will consist with the publick good) of every person in it."[30] Conversely, recognition of the need for prudence should not rule out conformity to such broad principles. In contrast to the currently influential dichotomy of idealism and realism, principle and prudence were complementary concepts for Locke and for the American founders.[31]

'The Federalist' on Justice and Power in Foreign Affairs

The duality of principle and prudence for the American founders can be seen most clearly in the familiar opening of the Declaration of Independence. The Declaration proclaims the general principles of human equality, individual rights, government by consent, and the right of revolution, but its very next word is "prudence," which dictates that governments long established should not be changed for light and transient causes. Both those principles and that prudence guide the fundamental act of American foreign policy, the assumption of that separate and equal station that entitles the United States to have full power to levy war, conclude peace, contract alliances, establish commerce, and do all other things that independent states may rightfully do. (Both also are relevant to the decisions made by foreign states concerning what relations to establish with the United States.)

The duality of principle and prudence can also be seen clearly in John Jay's discussion of justice and power in foreign affairs in *Federalist* Nos. 3 and 4. His consideration of the dangers of hostilities from abroad begins with the following remark:

> The number of wars which have happened or will happen in the world will always be found to be in proportion to the number and weight of the causes, whether *real* or *pretended*, which *provoke* or *invite* them.[32]

Jay's subsequent discussion makes clear that this remark means that wars are caused both by real or just and by pretended or unjust causes. They can result from unjust conduct on the part of one nation that provokes another into making war with a real or just cause as well as from weakness on the part of one nation that invites another to make war with only a pretended or unjust cause.[33] (Jay's initial remark is misleadingly formulated in that he turns out to mean that wars occur in proportion to the real weaknesses that invite other nations to allege pretended causes rather than in proportion to the pretended causes themselves—both kinds of effective causes are real rather than pretended.) In contrast both to the utopians who believe that justice is sufficient to keep the peace and fail to take strength seriously and to the cynics who believe that strength is sufficient and fail to take justice seriously, Jay takes both seriously. A nation needs both justice and power to keep the peace; either injustice or weakness can result in war.

Jay is neither more naive nor less realistic than the cynics who call themselves realists. He treats justice within the argument of *Federalist* No. 3 not as a virtue that is intrinsically attractive but as a means to

29

peace and safety. He presumes no disinterested dedication to obtaining justice for others; he merely recognizes that nations may resort to war when they are injured and not only when they have a prospect of getting anything by it. He suggests later in No. 3 that "a quick sense of apparent interest or injury" might lead the border states to acts of violence against adjacent Spanish or British territory, thereby provoking wars that prudence would avoid. He also notes in No. 4 that absolute monarchs make war for revenge for personal affronts, and Alexander Hamilton writes in No. 7 of wars to chastise "atrocious breaches of moral obligation and social justice."[34]

The Federalist's very first inquiry is therefore

> whether so many *just* causes of war are likely to be given by *united* America as by *disunited* America; for if it should turn out that united America will probably give the fewest, then it will follow that in this respect the Union tends most to preserve the people in a state of peace with other nations.[35]

Jay begins this paper by flattering the American people as "intelligent and well-informed" and therefore unlikely to be consistently mistaken about their own interests—they are not, however, consistently just and, therefore, likely to respect the rights of others. He flatters the people only to criticize them.[36] We cannot avoid being amazed by the spectacle of a statesman who expects to persuade the people with an argument that considers first how they might commit the fewest injustices. Jay's concern is not that Americans love wars and would deliberately start them (indeed he worries in the next paper that Americans may be "seduced by a too great fondness for peace"), but that his fellow countrymen would commit injustices and unwittingly provoke wars.[37]

Of the just causes of war (that is, the injustices that provoke other nations into making war with just cause), Jay considers first violations of treaties and the laws of nations. He warns that it is important to the peace of America that she observe her treaties and the laws of nations with those nations with which she has formed treaties or has extensive commerce. His argument that this will be "more perfectly and punctually done by one national government than it could be by either thirteen separate States or by three or four distinct confederacies" is clearly an argument not merely for the Union as against those hypothetical alternatives but for something like the Constitution rather than the Confederation. For he continues by contending that only "when once an efficient national government is established" (an event that unfortunately had not yet occurred) will "the best men in the country" be appointed and consent to manage it. Only then will the national government enjoy the services of men with more general and extensive reputation for talents and other qualifications in contrast to those men of only "town or country or other contracted influence" who manage the state governments. As a result its decisions will be "more wise, systematical, and judicious than those of individual States, and consequently more satisfactory with respect to other nations, as well as more *safe* with respect to us."[38]

The advantage in this respect of an efficient national government like that of the Constitution over that of the Confederation is twofold. Because it effectively makes national policy instead of letting the states go their own ways, it both attracts men repelled by impotence and frustration and it makes their decisions stick. Secretary Jay may not have expected the Constitution to provide a better secretary of foreign affairs than the Articles enjoyed—he may rather have expected its secretary to have the advantages of better bosses in the presidency and Senate than in the Congress of the Confederation. He emphasizes the consistency in interpretation of treaties and international law to be provided by the national judiciary he would soon head that was wisely provided by the Constitution and absent from the Confederation.

In considering both violations of treaties or of international law and direct violence (the other just cause of war), Jay propounds in *Federalist* No. 3 a version of the argument James Madison would make in No. 10.[39] He explains that "the prospect of present loss or advantage may often tempt the governing party in one or two States to swerve from good faith and justice" especially as such temptations commonly result from circumstances affecting a great number of the state's inhabitants. In contrast, the national government will not be affected by such local circumstances and could both resist such temptations and punish those in the states who succumb to them. Just as Madison argues in No. 10 that passions or interests adverse to the rights of other citizens or to the permanent and aggregate interests of the community are more likely to be confined to particular states than to pervade the whole body of the Union, so Jay concludes in No. 3 that the "passions and interests of a part" will more frequently occasion violence against Indians and foreign nations than would those of the whole. Distance from the borders in particular leaves the national government's wisdom and prudence less clouded by passion or biased by interests other than those of the whole.[40]

American violations of treaties and acts of violence were not merely hypothetical. Jay mentions "several instances of Indian hostilities having been provoked by the improper conduct of individual States." Hamilton in *Federalist* No. 15 complains:

> Are there engagements to the performance of which we are held by every tie respectable among men? These are the subjects of constant and unblushing violation.

He there laments that the "just imputations on our own faith" in respect to the peace treaty with Britain prevented the United States from being in "a condition to remonstrate with dignity" about British violations of the treaty.[41]

The distance between Jay's concern with justice and any naiveté is underlined by the limitation of his inquiry and of his answer. He asks only whether an efficient national government would commit and permit fewer injustices and concludes that it would. He does not claim that America can under any form of government expect to be perfectly just.

Because Jay expects some American injustice to occur in any case, he considers the national government's ability not only to prevent but also to punish its commission (presumably by states or private parties) and to acknowledge, correct, or repair such offenses. Not only will the national government's distance from the scene of the crime leave it "more temperate and cool" but its not having committed or permitted the crime in the first place will prevent its pride from interfering with apologies or reparations.[42]

Jay concludes No. 3 with a crucial twist that displays his subtle balance of justice and power. After pointing out the national government's greater willingness to repair American offenses against foreigners, he adds:

> Besides, it is well known that acknowledgments, explanations, and compensations are often accepted as satisfactory from a strong united nation, which would be rejected as unsatisfactory if offered by a State or confederacy of little consideration or power.

Jay wants America to commit as few injustices as possible, but because his country will in any case still commit some, he offers advice as to how to get away with it with as little humiliation or risk of war as possible. Justice matters but so do strength and unity.

Jay starts the argument of *Federalist* No. 4 accordingly by showing the insufficiency of justice to preserve the peace. He observes that

> the safety of the people of America against dangers from *foreign* force depends not only on their forbearing to give *just* causes of war to other nations, but also on their placing and

continuing themselves in such a situation as not to *invite* hostility or insult; for it need not be observed that there are *pretended* as well as just causes of war.

He explains the insufficiency of justice on the grounds that "nations in general will make war whenever they have a prospect of getting anything by it" and that absolute monarchs at least will "often make war when their nations are to get nothing by it." Jay admits that this may be disgraceful to human nature: the love of justice is not the strongest passion in the human breast, however bitter the resentment of injustice. Justice matters because injustice provokes nations to make war even when they expect to get nothing by it (other than the satisfaction of vindicating their rights), not because justice prevents nations in general from making war without just cause when they do expect to get anything by it. That this is only generally true, however, would permit America to try to be just even when she could get something by making war without just cause.[43]

In Jay's understanding, the causes of war are not simply a matter of human nature in general—forms of government make an important difference. Absolute monarchs often make wars for the sake of military glory, revenge for personal affronts, ambition, or dynastic connections. Republics or constitutional monarchs presumably are less frequently moved to war by such objects, although Jay says only that such inducements to war are "most prevalent" in absolute monarchies rather than peculiar to them. Jay says an absolute monarch often makes wars "not sanctified by justice or the voice and interests of his people," but he does not assume that the voice and interests of the people necessarily coincide with justice, either.[44]

Jay considers (without, as he notes, going into imprudent detail) how the particular situation and circumstances of America relative to other nations may give those nations inducements to make war and to find pretended causes to color and justify doing so. American commercial rivalry in the fisheries, in navigation and the carrying trade, in trade with China and India, and in trade with European colonies on or near our continent is bound to hurt the interests of European nations given American advantages of cheapness and excellence of productions, vicinity, and the "enterprise and address of our merchants and navigators." As a result, American "advancement in union, in power and consequence by land and by sea" will give rise to European jealousies and uneasiness. In short, European nations may resort to war against America to protect their commercial interests and from fear of the growth of American power.[45]

The lesson that Jay draws from even a just America's vulnerability to foreign hostility is that she must put herself in "*such a situation as,*" instead of *inviting* war, will tend to repress and discourage it," a situation consisting in "the best possible state of defense." He explains that the best possible state of defense that would tend to discourage unjust attacks is not a purely military matter but also political and economic. It "necessarily depends on the government, the arms, and the resources of the country." An effective national government that could better furnish and apply arms and better develop and direct resources would provide a better state of defense.[46]

Jay's argument helps to set the American pattern so familiar today in which the ability to wage war is conceived of solely in the context of the ability to deter war. He does not discuss American ability to prevail even in defensive war, let alone in offensive war founded upon reasons of state. To have argued for the Constitution or even the Union as the means to prevail in war would have played into the hands of the Anti-Federalists who charged the Federalists with a yen for military glory, for national grandeur, power, and splendor.[47]

The Union's advantage as Jay presents it here is not strictly limited, however, to serving peace through deterring war. The Union would also be better able to settle the terms of peace should deterrence fail.

Jay's argument contains an element of paradox. The cause of unjust attacks he singles out is other nations' jealousies of American "advancement in union, in power and consequence," but the solution he proffers is further unity and strength to deter attacks.[48] It seems, however, to be a combination of present weakness and division with growing strength and unity that excites both fear and contempt and thereby invites attack. Nonetheless, the transition Jay advocates would seem to be a moment of peculiar danger, and even afterward further advancement in American unity, power, and consequence might increase foreign jealousies and uneasiness and inducements to war. After all, Jay figures in *Federalist* No. 5 that division into several confederacies would lead whichever confederacy was distinguished by superior policy and good management to exceed the others in strength and consideration, excite their envy and fear, and tempt them to diminish its importance.[49] Union and power can provoke jealous attacks, but weakness and disunity offer no safe haven, either; perhaps the combination of justice and power would be least likely to arouse the fear and jealousy that lead to war.

Jay's balance of justice and power in the prevention of war indicates the need in the conduct of foreign affairs both for principled conformity to the rules of justice and for prudent acquisition and employment of power, the elements behind Locke's legislative and federative-executive powers.

'The Federalist' and the Foreign Affairs Power
under the Constitution

This recognition of the duality of justice and power, of principle and prudence, in foreign affairs elaborated in Nos. 3 and 4 also underlies *The Federalist*'s conception of the extent and character of the foreign affairs power of the new government under the Constitution.

In particular, *The Federalist* makes arguments for giving the federal government fiscal and defense powers free from constitutional limitations similar to those Locke makes for giving the executive the foreign affairs power free from direction by standing laws. The founders established a government limited in its ends and in some of its powers, but we should not forget the basic truth the Federalists insisted on and the Anti-Federalists fastened on, that it could raise as much money and as many men as it pleased.[50] Hamilton justifies these unlimited defense and fiscal powers in *Federalist* No. 23 in the following way:

> The authorities essential to the common defence are these: to raise armies; to build and equip fleets; to prescribe rules for the government of both; to direct their operations; to provide for their support. These powers ought to exist without limitation, *because it is impossible to foresee or to define the extent and variety of national exigencies, and the correspondent extent and variety of the means which may be necessary to satisfy them.* The circumstances that endanger the safety of nations are infinite, and for this reason no constitutional shackles can wisely be imposed on the power to which the care of it is committed.

Because the danger arising from foreign actions is in principle infinite, the defense power must be unlimited. The peculiar nature of foreign affairs makes the powers related to it peculiarly resistant to constitutional limitation. Hamilton's argument continues:

> unless it can be shown that the circumstances which may affect the public safety are reducible within certain determinate limits . . . it must be admitted as a necessary consequence that there can be no limitation of that authority which is to provide for the defense and protection of the community in any matter essential to its efficacy.[51]

Hamilton argues for the federal government's unlimited power to tax on the same basis in *Federalist* No. 31:

> As the duties of superintending the national defense and of securing the public peace against foreign or domestic vio-

lence involve a provision for casualties and dangers to which no possible limits can be assigned, the power of making that provision ought to know no other bounds than the exigencies of the nation and the resources of the community.[52]

That is, the only limit that can be safely assigned to how much a government can tax is *as much as it can*. Indeed, Hamilton admits with startling candor in *Federalist* No. 30 that a country's government will always need to spend at least as much money as the country has.[53]

Hamilton demonstrates the imprudence of limiting the federal government's fiscal powers by asking his readers to "attend to what would be the effects of this situation in the very first war in which we should happen to be engaged"—public credit would be destroyed. Foreign affairs and foreign danger are decisive (and the phrase "the very first war" suggests there will be many). He warns that Americans cannot "hope to see realized in America the halcyon scenes of the poetic or fabulous age," but must expect to "experience a common portion of the vicissitudes and calamities which have fallen to the lot of other nations."[54] He asks, "What are the chief sources of expense in every government?" and answers, "Wars and rebellions." Americans must, he insists, "calculate on a common share of the events which disturb the peace of nations." This would be necessary, Hamilton declares, even if Americans were to "try the novel and absurd experiment in politics of tying up the hands of government from offensive war founded upon reasons of state." (Hamilton regards it as absurd to preclude any government from being able sometimes to strike first against dangerous enemies for reasons of state rather than in strict response to injuries.)[55]

Hamilton makes the most striking version of this argument against constitutional limitation of powers necessary to cope with foreign danger in the mundane context of poll taxes:

> There are certain emergencies of nations in which expedients that in the ordinary state of things ought to be forborne become essential to the public weal. And the government, from the possibility of such emergencies, ought ever to have the option of making use of them. . . . And as I know nothing to exempt this portion of the globe from the common calamities that have befallen other parts of it, I acknowledge my aversion to every project that is calculated to disarm the government of a single weapon, which in any possible contingency might be usefully employed for the general defense and security.[56]

It seems to be above all the nature of foreign affairs and foreign danger that resists limits not only on fiscal power but on any power that could be a useful weapon in a national emergency.

This argument for unlimited federal fiscal and defense powers on the basis of the infinite character of foreign danger is made by Madison as well. In *Federalist* No. 41, Madison writes:

> With what color or propriety could the force necessary for defence be limited by those who cannot limit the force of offence? If a federal Constitution could chain the ambition or set bounds to the exertions of all other nations, then indeed might it prudently chain the discretion of its own government, and set bounds to the exertions for its own safety.
>
> How could a readiness for war in time of peace be safely prohibited, unless we could prohibit, in like manner, the preparations and establishments of every hostile nation? The means of security can only be regulated by the means and the danger of attack. They will, in fact, be ever determined by these rules, and by no others. It is in vain to oppose constitutional barriers to the impulse of self-preservation.[57]

In other words, a government must be able to do whatever is necessary to counter foreign actions; no constitutional provision can prevent that. Such decisions must be made not by imprudently inflexible constitutional provisions but by prudential judgments in response to shifting circumstances. The Constitution must itself be prudent in leaving room for prudence.

Hamilton does not deny that this resistance of the defense power to constitutional limitation could pose dangers to liberty. He admits candidly in No. 26 that

> if the defense of the community . . . should make it necessary to have an army so numerous as to hazard its liberty, this is one of those calamities for which there is neither preventative nor cure. It cannot be provided against by any possible form of government.

He did, however, oppose that narrow or doctrinaire view of free or republican or federal government, which would render it by definition incapable of effective conduct of foreign affairs, as the Anti-Federalist insistence on constitutional limitation of power in disregard of foreign danger seemed to do. The Federalists, in contrast, sought to redefine free, republican, and federal government in an effort to meet that challenge. In particular, Hamilton sees in the frequent Anti-Federalist demand that the Constitution prohibit a standing army in time of peace the view that "All that kind of policy by which nations anticipate distant danger and meet the gathering storm must be abstained from, as contrary to the genuine maxims of a free government." Free nations, to preserve their freedom, must like any others have the flexibility of power to prepare for war in time of peace in order to preserve peace or prevail in war.[58]

In all these passages *The Federalist* argues from unlimited foreign danger for unlimited power but in a context significantly different from that in which Locke had done so. Whereas Locke advocated leaving the conduct of the foreign affairs power to the prudence of the executive, free from direction by standing laws made by the legislative, *The Federalist* advocates leaving the extent of the essential foreign affairs powers to the prudence of the federal government (especially, in the cases under consideration, its legislative power), free from direction by constitutional limitations made by the people. These arguments do not explicitly affect the division of the foreign affairs power between the legislative and executive branches.

The Federalist's arguments against constitutional limitation of the essential foreign affairs powers do, however, indicate a conception of that power as an unlimitable capability to deal with unlimitable contingencies—a conception that can in turn also justify leaving the conduct by the executive of the foreign affairs power free from direction by standing laws made by the legislative power. That possibility leaves open again legislative control other than by standing laws. The legislature, however, is designed for the purpose of making general laws rather than occasional judgments founded on present circumstances.

The need in foreign affairs for justice as well as power, for conformity to principle as well as management by prudence, suggests, however, a role for legislative direction, albeit not a role reducible within certain determinate limits, as well as a role for executive discretion. The legislature does not have the same relation to the principles of justice governing foreign affairs as it does to those governing domestic affairs—it is not elected by all those whose rights may be at stake. Nevertheless, the Senate, especially, is supposed to provide our foreign policy with stability, a concern for reputation abroad, and a systematic character, the concomitants of conformity to principle.[59] The president is supposed to provide secrecy and dispatch, the concomitants of prudent management.[60]

The dual share of the executive and the legislature in foreign policy is related, though not in a simple, one-to-one correspondence, to the duality of principle and prudence in foreign affairs. The legislature will tend to invoke the need for conformity to principle in its efforts to subordinate the executive's conduct of foreign policy to legislative direction; the executive will tend to invoke the need for prudent management in response to foreign actions in its efforts to resist legislative direction—although there may be cases where the positions are really or ostensibly reversed. The need for executive discretion in response to varying circumstances will itself vary with circumstances. In times of danger, there will be more of a share for the executive. In peaceful times, there will be more of a share for the legislature. The division can never be resolved neatly.

3
Reflections on the Role of the Judiciary in Foreign Policy
Michael M. Uhlmann

"Where does the Constitution lodge the power to determine the foreign relations of the United States?"[1] That deceptively simple question is posed by Professor Corwin in his famous treatise on the office and powers of the president. His answer runs the better part of 100 pages of text, plus 50 pages of small-print, discursive footnotes—all this in a general guide to the main features of the presidency. Corwin's question, in one form or another, has caused animated, indeed passionate debate since the 1790s and has spawned a literature commensurate in size with the importance of the subject.[2]

Hamilton versus Madison

That question retains its vitality during the 1980s. We should not despair, however, if we are unable to provide a succinct answer—nor should we despair, for that matter, if we fail to advance the argument much beyond the confines of the exchange between Alexander Hamilton and James Madison in 1793. In that year those eminent worthies squared off at twenty paces over the legality of President Washington's Proclamation of Neutrality, which he had issued to prevent the new nation from becoming involved in the European wars.[3]

Hamilton's argument, in a nutshell, was that foreign affairs are an inherently executive function; that Article II of the Constitution, in vesting "the executive Power" in the president, meant to bestow all rights and privileges pertaining to the nature of the power, including the right to control foreign policy; that the subsequent grants of specific powers to the president illustrate, rather than limit, the general grants of executive power; and that, absent express restriction in the Constitution, the power of presidential control is to be presumed.

Spurred by an almost frantic Jefferson[4]—he would not be the last secretary of state to oppose the policies of his own chief—Madison replied that the Constitution, in vesting the power to declare war in Congress, thereby bestowed the right to manage the foreign policy of the United States; that the president's powers in the area are ministerial, or essentially executory in the narrow sense; and that any exceptions to the grant of war-making authority to Congress are to be construed strictly against the president.

In this exchange between these two towering figures—each of whom must be supposed to know what he was talking about—may be found the seeds of virtually all subsequent constitutional debate on the question. Partisans of each position—and of every position in between—may be found today, as they may be found throughout American history, and their arguments retain the political passion (even if they sometimes lack the nobility) of the original debate. One may lament the imprecision of the Constitution on this subject in the manner of Justice Jackson, who thought it "almost as enigmatic as the dreams Joseph was called upon to interpret for Pharaoh,"[5] or one may lament the inability of subsequent political experience to settle the issue with compelling finality. The beginning of wisdom on the subject, however, is to seek no more certainty than the nature of the matter under inquiry admits. The nature of the matter here is difficult not only because the Constitution is silent on certain crucial questions; not only because it brings into sharp relief the irreducible tension between the legislature and the executive; not only because one must deliberate about the meaning of that most opaque of constitutional phrases, "the executive Power"; but because in thinking about the nature and distribution of foreign policy powers in the Constitution, one is sooner or later forced to consider whether a particular construction will enable the nation to endure—and endure not just in the sense of survival but as a nation whose governors rule with the consent of the governed.

It is that last consideration which makes the 200-year-old debate about the power to control foreign affairs so complicated, so passionate, so rewarding, so unending. One mistakes the character of the exchange between Hamilton and Madison if one reduces it to a lawyers' dispute over the meaning of arcane terms of art or to a dispute in which constitutional phrases are mere rhetorical masks for hidden motives. At the heart of this debate is the desire to ensure two objectives at once: popular sovereignty and national survival. The effort to secure these goals must guard against the opposite vices of deficiency and excess. The danger is that popular sentiment may be so indifferent or so inflamed, or the government so enfeebled or so tyrannical, as to make national policy inefficient or undemocratic or both. Whatever our other differences, surely we can agree that the

41

Constitution was intended to be, and should be read as, an instrument capable of meeting every exigency that the concatenation of chance events can present and that its highest purpose is the execution of policy that is at once efficacious and informed by popular consent. This is the spirit that unites disputants despite their other disagreements. This same spirit has animated the Supreme Court in its several major efforts to grapple with the emanations of Professor Corwin's deceptively simple question.

Judicial Hesitancy

As Tocqueville remarked, our system tends to resolve all political disputes, sooner or later, into judicial disputes.[6] That observation, however, applies less in the area of foreign affairs than perhaps in any other. The inhospitality of the courts, or at least of the Supreme Court, to actions arising under the Constitution's foreign relations powers frustrates many, especially professors and members of Congress in opposition to the president. After all, they argue, did not the great Chief Justice Marshall lay it down once and for all that "it is emphatically, the province and duty of the judicial department to say what the law is"?[7] Is the protection of individual rights or the preservation of the separation of powers any less a duty because the source of the injury is foreign as opposed to domestic policy? Certainly nothing in the constitutional provisions empowering the judiciary suggests that the courts' jurisdiction is less potent in the one area than in the other; to the contrary, Article III presents a number of express jurisdictional opportunities for judicial involvement in foreign affairs. Why then the hesitancy?

The answer, at once subtle and complicated, deserves more extensive treatment than can be devoted to it here. Suffice it to say here that the hesitancy is a product of factual circumstance and, more important, of the Supreme Court's considered sense of its own role. Typically, judicial power is invoked when a private party alleges that individual rights have been infringed by some action or inaction by the government. That pattern is not unknown in the field of foreign affairs, but it is not common. More commonly, the aggrieved party's primary interest lies less in the redress of personal grievances than in the alteration or reversal of a disagreeable policy. Even with a plausible statutory or constitutional claim of right, a party immediately encounters a formidable array of obstacles in the form of objections based on standing, ripeness, and the political questions doctrine (to name only three). And even if those hurdles are surmounted, the Court may hesitate to proceed as it might were the dispute wholly or predominantly domestic in nature—and for good reason. Much of the world of international relations is *terra incognita* to the judiciary; indeed it is often *terra incognita* even to those who make it their profession. It is a world ruled by King Contingency, where caprice, deceit, and passion dominate far more than order, honor, and reason. It is a world where "ignorant armies clash by night"; a world where accurate information is hard to come by and often secretly acquired; a world where the consequences of mistakes are long-lived and frequently fatal.

Little in the training or experience of the judiciary equips it to dispose of such matters as it disposes of domestic issues. It possesses even less capacity to predict the outcome of its judgments. If that were not enough, the courts must surely recognize that foreign policy disputes tend to be partisan disputes—the more partisan, the more passionate, and the more passionate, the less susceptible to resolution by the main instrument of the courts' power, namely, reason.

Further, the judiciary knows or ought to know that in foreign policy disputes, constitutional issues of the most dramatic sort are seldom far from the heart of the matter. If the issue involves the separation of powers and if the merits of the case are considered, a court will inevitably find itself questioning the self-proclaimed and highly prized prerogatives of one of the political branches. In any event, as the only party who can do much about changing the execution of a challenged policy is the president, a court must face the daunting prospect of ordering the chief executive to do something that his considered view of the state of the world—not to mention of his oath of office—strongly disinclines him to do.

Finally, the judiciary cannot be unmindful of its own vital interests in the constitutional scheme. In the field of foreign relations, those interests may have less to do with the assertion of power than with "the inner vulnerability, the self-doubt of an institution which is electorally irresponsible and has no earth to draw strength from."[8]

For whatever reasons, the Supreme Court has evinced a studied reluctance to engage in foreign policy debates, especially when the political branches are at swords' points. In contrast to domestic policy, where the Court has been anything but a reluctant participant, the cases suggest a certain institutional timidity. This is true even where the judiciary has been most active, namely, the law involving treaties. Here we have a fairly well-developed body of judge-made law, touching such subjects as the relationship of treaties to acts of Congress[9] and the powers of the states;[10] the powers of Congress vis-à-vis those of the president;[11] the nature and extent of constitutional limitations upon the treaty power;[12] and the status of executive agreements.[13]

Even here, however, the reluctance to assert the full range of judicial powers is apparent although subject matter jurisdiction is nevertheless authorized by both Constitution and statute, and the supremacy clause places treaties on the same footing with statutory enactments.[14]

Notwithstanding general statements in Court decisions, for example, the Court has never, without the assent of Congress, given full force and effect to a treaty inconsistent with a prior act of Congress.[15] It is even unclear to what extent the Bill of Rights limits the exercise of the treaty power.[16] More recently, the Court refused to take on the still unresolved and interesting question whether the president, acting alone, may terminate a treaty.[17] In short, even where the Constitution is clear in authorizing jurisdiction, and where the judiciary has a nearly 200-year-old tradition of judge-made law to rely upon, the Court treads carefully.

Presidential Interpretation and Action

Although it is error to suppose, as Justice Brennan said in a much-quoted opinion on the political questions doctrine, "that every case or controversy which touches foreign relations lies beyond judicial cognizance,"[18] it is also true, as then–Chief Justice Burger said in another case, that matters "intimately related to foreign policy and national security are rarely proper subjects for judicial intervention."[19] Similar contrasting sentiments can be produced almost at will from a random sampling of Supreme Court cases dealing—or refusing to deal—with foreign policy questions. If the Court appears to be of more than one mind when deciding whether the judicial power should be invoked in these disputes, it nevertheless seems to be fairly well-settled on the nature of the president's powers. Whatever one's opinion on the original understanding of the framers, whatever one may think of the subsequent gloss applied by Hamilton and Madison, the weight of history has confirmed the essence of the Hamiltonian view. As Professor Charles Lofgren pointed out in a fine essay on the subject, "while Congress and others have debated, Presidents have acted."[20]

A frequent argument contends that although presidential action must be acknowledged as a matter of fact, it has usurped congressional power as a matter of law. That view has great appeal, as a long and thoughtful literature attests. Upon deeper reflection, however, the issue may be less a question of usurpation than an inexorable unfolding of ideas that were implicit all along in the idea of the executive. Much has been made of the last-minute appearance of the phrase "executive Power"—inserted by the Committee on Style without prior deliberation—during the Constitutional Convention. That fact, in turn, throws the diviners of original intent back to Locke, Montesquieu, and Blackstone with interesting but hardly dispositive results. In any event, we would do well to remember that the world—including the framers of the Constitution—had never before seen anything like a *republican* executive. For that reason alone, prior experience and commentary are less useful than they might otherwise be as guides to our understanding. In short, the idea of the executive as set forth in the Constitution is not exactly an experiment but it is something close to it.

Subsequent events, happily, confirm this experiment as an outstanding success, and history has thus blessed us with a meaning that even the most careful reading of the original design has been unable to yield. That meaning is no mere creature of chance events or presidential contrivance, as if the major actors were motivated simply or primarily by a desire for power. It is in large part a product of mature reflection by our leading statesmen, honed by their experience in office. Although this influence is a subject for another time and place, we would rob this discussion of much needed light if we failed to mention how much the presidential office and our understanding of it have been shaped by its most memorable occupants, especially during the first fourscore and seven years of the nation's history—most notably, Washington, Jefferson, Jackson, and Lincoln. Our opinings about the meaning of executive power do not occur in a vacuum, nor do they consist merely of variations of what Bagehot called the "literary theory" of the Constitution. They are formed decisively by the reflections of men who understood themselves not as would-be despots but as *republican* chief executives, holding office under and through a form of government that derives its just powers from the consent of the governed. In a sense, our greatest presidents may rightly be said to have "created" the office; in doing so, they were inspired by a Constitution that instructed them about the kind of office it ought to be.

Ratification of Hamilton's Concept

We have every reason to believe that the opinings of the Supreme Court itself have been formed by the same experience, even as they contribute in their own way to a refinement of that experience. Although the Court's participation in foreign policy debate is limited as compared with its participation in domestic policy, it has contributed mightily to our understanding of the constitutional status of the executive's diplomatic and military powers. Much of this constitutional jurisprudence, at least in larger conceptualization, is a twentieth-century phenomenon, a fact altogether befitting the growth of the United States as a world power. In *Myers* v. *United States*,[21] decided in 1926, the Court in effect gave final ratification to Hamilton's concept of inherent presidential power, a concept that had long since been ratified by presidential action and, more important, by the court of public opinion. Appropriately enough, the Court's opinion in *Myers* was written by the only man who enjoyed the honor of serving as head of two branches of government. Chief Justice Taft, in adopting Hamilton's latitudinarian reading of Article II, stated, "The executive power was given in general terms, strengthened by specific terms where emphasis was regarded as appropriate, and was limited by direct expressions where limitation was needed. . . ."[22] As long as the activity in question may be rightly understood as executive in nature, said Taft, the president's authority is implied unless expressly limited.

As *Myers* was principally concerned with the removal power, its implications for foreign policy were necessarily indirect, although significant. The opinion did not deal, for example, with the question of the executive's relation to Congress in respect of shared foreign policy powers. Ten years later, however, Justice Sutherland filled at least part of the void in *United States* v. *Curtiss-Wright Export Corp.*[23] The case arose on appeal from an indictment for violation of a presidentially declared arms embargo. A joint resolution of Congress had empowered the president to declare an embargo if he found that the sale of arms would prolong a South American war. The narrow question before the Court concerned the constitutionality of the congressional delegation to the president, which Sutherland quickly settled in the affirmative. He took the occasion, however, to expound his views (in which all but one colleague joined) on the nature of the foreign relations power in general and the president's constitutional role in particular. In words that have ever since warmed the hearts of proponents of the executive power, he noted:

> Not only, as we have shown, is the federal power over external affairs in origin and essential character different from that over internal affairs, but participation in the exercise of the power is significantly limited. In this vast external realm, with its important, complicated, delicate and manifold problems, the President alone has the power to speak or listen as a representative of the nation. He *makes* treaties with the advice and consent of the Senate; but he alone negotiates. Into the field of negotiations the Senate cannot intrude; and Congress itself is powerless to invade it.[24]

Sutherland distinguished sharply between the chief executive's more limited implied power to act in domestic matters and his more expansive implied power to act on his own authority and discretion in the nation's dealings abroad. The breadth of presidential discretion, he suggested, was required by the nature of the activity in question and derived from the Constitution itself rather than from any grant of legislative power:

> It is important to bear in mind that we are here dealing not alone with an authority vested in the President by an exertion of legislative power, but with such an authority plus the very delicate, plenary and exclusive power of the President as the sole organ of the federal government in the field of international relations—a power which does not require as a basis for its exercise an act of Congress, but which, of course, like every other governmental power, must be exercised in subordination to the applicable provisions of the Constitution. It is quite apparent that if, in the maintenance of our international relations, embarrassment—perhaps serious embarrassment—is to be avoided and success for our aims achieved, congressional legislation which is to be made effective through negotiation and inquiry within the international field must often accord to the President a degree of discretion and freedom from statutory restriction which would not be admissible were domestic affairs alone involved.[25]

Certain aspects of Sutherland's opinion have been severely criticized by scholars, particularly his theory that the power to conduct international relations passed to the United States government not from the Constitution but from the British Crown.[26] The fragility of his theory of national sovereignty and its origins notwithstanding, the other emanations of Sutherland's opinion concerning the nature of the executive power remain largely intact. Significantly, the Supreme Court has never denied them.

Curtiss-Wright can be understood in a number of ways, as Charles Lofgren, among others, has shown.[27] At one extreme, it can be read narrowly as certifying maximum discretionary power in the president only or primarily when it is exercised pursuant to an act of Congress—as in *Curtiss-Wright*. At the other extreme, it can be read as an endorsement of that discretion with or without express congressional authorization. While scholars and others have debated these polar positions (and virtually everything in between), events have tended to ratify a more expansive view of the *Curtiss-Wright* holding. In its immediate aftermath, certainly, it provided important support for Franklin Roosevelt's assertion of executive power before our formal entry into World War II, including, most prominently, the Declaration of Panama, the destroyer-base agreement with Great Britain, and the promulgation of the Atlantic Charter. Because of the scope of these agreements, any traditional understanding of the relationship between Congress and the president would have required some sort of legislative authority in the form of either a treaty ratification or more general implementing legislation. Roosevelt, however, sought neither because he deemed it unnecessary as a matter of law (and given the mood of Congress, probably impolitic as well).

The destroyer agreement of September 1940 was in constitutional terms perhaps Roosevelt's boldest move because it flew in the face of an express congressional enactment to the contrary. The agreement was justified in an opinion by then–Attorney General Jackson that rested on an exceedingly artful piece of legislative interpretation: in essence, Jackson read a statute to mean exactly the opposite of what Congress clearly intended. Roosevelt's action and Jackson's opinion brought forth a scathing attack from, among others, Professor Corwin, who called the agreement "an endorsement of unrestrained autocracy in the field of our foreign relations," and said of Jackson's legal rationale that "no such dangerous opinion was ever before penned by an Attorney-General of the United States."[28]

Congress, however, failed to rise in its wrath because Roosevelt's action prevailed in the court of public opinon. (Apparently no one thought to invoke the judicial power to resolve this arguably unconstitutional exertion of presidential prerogative, which says something about the then-prevailing view of the role of judiciary.) Roosevelt, it is true, was nothing if not a master of securing his political base; in this, perhaps his finest hour, he later sought and was given legislative support in the prewar years for a wide range of activities that were notable chiefly for the extraordinary breadth of authority they delegated to the president.

Roosevelt's prewar leadership might have been sustained without benefit of the *Curtiss-Wright* doctrine. There was, after all, some precedent for his behavior in the actions of a number of his predecessors, chiefly Lincoln and Wilson. But there is no doubt that *Curtiss-Wright*, by affirming the breadth of presidential discretion in foreign affairs, provided him with a constitutional rationale, one that presidents ever since have relied upon as authority for their behavior.

With or without *Curtiss-Wright*, however, Roosevelt's prewar actions might have led to a major constitutional confrontation between Congress and the president, had they not later been dissolved by our formal entry into the war. Whether in that event there was anything the Supreme Court could or should have done, I leave for another occasion.

I dwell here on Roosevelt's behavior in the years immediately before World War II to draw into sharp relief the kinds of difficulties the Court faces when it attempts to assert its reach over the subject matter of foreign relations, especially at moments of arguable national emergency. The Court is caught on the horns of a dilemma: it must either limit the reach of the undoubted constitutional power to legislate or second-guess the judgment of the president, who, by the nature of his office, claims not only the constitutional power but also the factual base requisite to intelligent judgment. The outcome cannot be happy either way—for Congress, the president, the Court, or the Constitution.

Youngstown Steel and the Separation of Powers

Perhaps the most notable venture of the Court onto this unhappy ground occurred in the *Youngstown Steel* case.[29] The Court ruled, six to three, against President Truman's seizure of the steel mills to prevent a threatened strike during the Korean War, but no theory of the case was able to command a majority. Justice Black wrote a plurality opinion, in which he denied the existence of inherent presidential power. Four of his brethren, however, seemed to place primary emphasis on the fact that Truman acted in opposition to clearly expressed legislation to the contrary; one could argue that they would have voted differently in the absence of contrary statutory expression. Along the way, Justice Jackson contributed his famous three-part test for judging the constitutionality of inherent presidential power (that is, action pursuant to, contrary to, or in the absence of congressional authority). Three justices voted to support the president.

The Court's judgment made clear that President Truman lacked constitutional authority for his actions, but almost everything else was unclear, or at least arguable, and has remained so to this day. Seven of the nine members of the Court, however, conceded in principle the existence of inherent executive power. As to the circumstances under which that power can be validly exercised, only the law reviews know for sure. Even at the remove of thirty-seven years, the precedential value of the case remains problematic, although we are surely richer for the Court's troubled deliberations. Clearly, a majority of the Court was of the view that a genuine national emergency did not exist, but we have no legal criteria to guide us toward defining the real thing. Presumably, that is why we have presidents—and a Congress to keep them in check.

The *Youngstown Steel* case cannot have been a pleasant undertaking for the Court. Here was the president of the United States asserting his considered judgment that continued steel production was vital to the supply of arms in an ongoing war and that a strike would "immediately jeopardize our national defense."[30] On the other side, ultimately, were arrayed the considerable legislative powers of Article I, which argued that Congress, and Congress alone, could authorize what the president had done and that, lacking such authorization, the president was acting unconstitutionally. The Court's mighty efforts to resolve this confrontation were unavailing to almost all concerned. It made clear that inherent presidential power was not unlimited power, but we already knew that. Justice Black's embrace of Madison's Whiggish view of executive power commanded only his own vote and that of Justice Douglas. Three members of the Court said that the president's actions were lawful, and the remaining four said, in effect, that it was a close call. In the end, however, we are no closer to a workable test for determining where the powers of Congress end and those of the president begin than we were at the outset. The final word, perhaps, was stated by Justice Jackson, who said that in the absence of either a congressional grant or denial of authority, "any actual test of power is likely to depend on the imperatives of events and contemporary imponderables rather than on abstract theories of law."[31]

Youngstown Steel thrust the Court against the ultimate meaning of the separation of powers and against the implicit proposition that exigencies of political life can test the limits of the rule of law. It thereby brought the Court to the limits of its own institutional powers. Perhaps that is why in the intervening years the so-called political questions doctrine has received so much attention in the field of foreign relations. The issues raised by the doctrine cannot receive any more than cursory examination here, but by way of background, the Court over the years has articulated a number of rules whereby the judiciary can sidestep the merits of certain kinds of cases or controversies. Among them are considerations of standing, ripeness, mootness, and political questions—considerations sometimes based on a sense of institutional propriety, sometimes derived from the Constitution itself.[32]

In its initial formulation at the hands of John Marshall, the political questions doctrine held that judicial review is inappropriate where the Constitution has committed the resolution of the issues to the political branches.[33] His statement of the rule and his reliance on the separation of powers as its ultimate ground have been ratified by the Court on numerous occasions, with some frequency in the field of foreign relations. At times, the Court has dismissed cases on this basis and noted the particular branch to which the Constitution committed the issue,[34] but it has also done so without deciding whether Congress or the president has the constitutional power to decide the matter.[35]

The most interesting and recent case of the latter type was *Goldwater* v. *Carter,* which the Court confronted in 1979. Senator Goldwater had filed suit arguing that without the advice and consent of the Senate, President Carter could not terminate a treaty with the government of Taiwan. The Court dismissed the case as a nonjusticiable political question, but no rationale could muster a majority. Justice Rehnquist, writing for a plurality of four, adopted a broad view of the political questions doctrine "because it involves the authority of the President in the conduct of our country's foreign relations and the extent to which the Senate or the Congress is authorized to negate the action of the President."[36] He specifically distinguished *Youngstown Steel,* on which Goldwater had relied, on the grounds (a) that the petitioners there were *private* litigants and (b) that the president's action was one of "profound and demonstrable *domestic* impact" (emphasis added). He continued:

> Here, by contrast, we are asked to settle a dispute between coequal branches of our Government, each of which has resources available to protect and assert its interests, resources not available to private litigants outside the judicial forum.[37]

Rehnquist's position, which came one vote shy of commanding a majority of the Court, has been the occasion of (even as it reflects) a widespread debate.[38] With the subsequent change in membership on the Court, it will be interesting to see whether his view will enjoy a richer life.

Future Challenges to the Executive

The Court may not want for an opportunity, given the frequency with which members of Congress now seek to invoke the judicial power in their disputes with the president over foreign policy.[39] A recent case may afford an example of things to come. In 1987, 110 members of the House of Representatives and three members of the Senate filed suit in Federal District Court in Washington, D.C., arguing that President Reagan violated the War Powers Resolution by failing to file a report concerning incidents in the Persian Gulf.[40] They asked the court to order the president to submit a report. The president responded by arguing that the doctrines of standing, political questions, and equitable discretion all precluded judicial review.

The court sidestepped the standing question and dismissed the case on the other two grounds. In the context of exercising equitable discretion, the court noted that the plaintiff's dispute was primarily with their fellow legislators:

51

> This Court declines to accept jurisdiction to render a decision that, regardless of its substance, would impose a consensus on Congress. Congress is free to adopt a variety of positions on the War Powers Resolution, depending on its ability to achieve a political consensus. If the Court were to intervene in this political process, it would be acting "beyond the limits inherent in the [c]onstitutional scheme." Moreover, in view of a sponsor's statements that the determination of "hostilities" under the War Powers Resolution is a question for the executive and legislative branches, federal jurisdiction would be especially inappropriate in this case.[41]

The court expressly noted, however, that judicial review of the War Powers Resolution was not precluded by its decision: "A true confrontation between the Executive and a unified Congress, as evidenced by its passage of legislation to enforce the Resolution, would pose a question ripe for judicial review."[42]

With that by way of predicate, the court embraced the political questions doctrine on prudential rather than on constitutional grounds but noted that had the constitutionality of the War Powers Resolution been squarely presented, those considerations would not have been relevant.[43] An open invitation, thus, has been extended by a federal court.

Conclusion

In the nearly 200 years since the Hamilton-Madison argument over President Washington's Neutrality Proclamation, the Supreme Court has frequently blessed the Hamiltonian conception of the presidency. It has done so at times broadly and explicitly and at other times narrowly and implicitly. The cases demonstrate, if nothing else, that there are many mansions in the house of Hamilton. However one reads the cases, the Court has never embraced the errand-boy or merely ministerial conception of the presidency that is logically implicit in Madison's position—a conception that, ironically, Congress was only too willing to impose on Madison during his own unhappy presidency. There are dangers to an unbridled Hamiltonian understanding of the executive power, but there is no reason to believe that the Court has been blind to them.

Although those dangers are never to be regarded lightly, the risk in our time may lie elsewhere. With the political branches controlled by opposition parties, sharp political fights between Congress and the president over foreign policy have become an everyday occurrence. Much to the chagrin of recent presidents, Congress has not hesitated to impose increasingly detailed terms and conditions on the conduct of foreign policy by the executive. This has occurred more or less simultaneously with an expansion of federal judicial power, which itself is highly controversial. That expansion may reflect little more than the growth of government to the point where it regulates, or can regulate, virtually every aspect of human life. Thus far, the judiciary has not systematically asserted power over foreign affairs of the sort it has come to exercise with some frequency over domestic affairs. But if Congress is disposed to regulate the details of the president's conduct of international relations as it has recently, the courts may find themselves drawn willy-nilly into a major constitutional controversy, the seeds of which have clearly been planted.

What the Supreme Court can or should do when and if those seeds reach full flower is a question on which intelligent differences of opinion can be entertained. But at such moments, it is good to be reminded of Tocqueville's words, published in 1835:

> The peace, prosperity and very existence of the Union rest continually in the hands of these seven [now nine] federal judges. Without them the Constitution would be a dead letter; it is to them that the executive appeals to resist the encroachments of the legislative body, the legislature to defend itself against the assaults of the executive, the Union to make the states obey it, the States to rebuff the exaggerated pretensions of the Union, public interest against private interest, the spirit of conservation against democratic instability. Their power is immense, but it is power springing from opinion. They are all-powerful so long as the people consent to obey the law; they can do nothing when they scorn it. Now, of all powers, that of opinion is the hardest to use, for it is impossible to say exactly where its limits come. Often it is as dangerous to lag behind as to outstrip it.
>
> The federal judges therefore must not only be good citizens and men of education and integrity, qualities necessary for all magistrates, but must also be statesmen; they must know how to understand the spirit of the age, to confront those obstacles that can be overcome, and to steer out of the current when the tide threatens to carry them away, and with them the sovereignty of the Union and obedience to its laws.[44]

4

Foreign Trade
and the Constitution

Jacques J. Gorlin

When on August 23, 1988, President Ronald Reagan signed the Omnibus Trade and Competitiveness Act of 1988, he took exception to some of the provisions of the 1,000-page bill, calling them "inconsistent with our constitutional principles."[1] The president was reacting to provisions in the bill that Congress had inserted "to reduce [his] trade powers and to reassert its constitutional authority to regulate foreign commerce."[2] Notwithstanding this division over constitutional prerogatives, both the executive and the legislative branches recognize their shared responsibility for foreign trade policy. Three years earlier the president had invited Congress to work with him "to put into place any necessary legislation that would help us promote free and fair trade."[3] During floor debate on the resultant bill, Senator Lloyd Bentsen, chairman of the Senate Finance Committee, declared that neither the president nor the Congress would write the bill alone, but "it is a consensus we arrive at in a democratic process. The Congress has a shared responsibility in trade. It is not for us to negotiate, but it is for us to be a part of setting the policy."[4]

This consensus view of the shared responsibility in foreign trade masks the fact that the constitutional supremacy of Congress in foreign trade is unambiguous. The Constitution clearly gives Congress the authority, in Article I, section 8, "to regulate Commerce with foreign Nations." The relationship between this congressional authority and the president's general executive power, under Article II, section 1, and the Constitution's charge that he "take care that the Laws be faithfully executed" (Article II, section 3) has been well established in the 200-year history of the Republic.

The consensus on the shared responsibility in foreign trade also differentiates debates on trade policy from those over other foreign policy issues. National debates over such international political issues as the commitment of troops abroad are heavily punctuated by questions over who has the constitutional authority to set the policy and how that authority affects the conduct of particular actions. The Gulf of Tonkin Resolution of 1964, which President Lyndon B. Johnson used as evidence of congressional support for his Vietnam War policies, and the War Powers Resolution of 1973 were attempts to deal with the ambiguities rooted in the Constitution on how the United States conducts a military action abroad.[5] Neither was successful, however, in putting to rest the constitutional debate.

National debates over U.S. trade policy are not constitutional. The constitutional issues related to foreign trade have been resolved,[6] and the debates are concerned with substantive policy issues and the conditions for the delegation of congressional authority over trade to the executive for its implementation of the policy. References to the Constitution in trade debates are only used as adjuncts in support of positions on substantive policy.

The shared responsibility for U.S. trade policy creates a mutual dependence that puts a premium on ensuring that the policy process functions properly. Congress, for its part, depends on the executive to implement its constitutional function; the executive depends on periodic congressional delegations of authority to function in the international arena.

Notwithstanding the practice of shared responsibility, the unambiguous constitutional supremacy of Congress in foreign trade essentially means that the process of setting policy is legislatively based. The usual relationship of policy and legislation is altered. Although the trade policy of the United States is more than just the trade legislation enacted by Congress and signed by the president, U.S. trade law must be the vehicle for policy articulation in a system dominated by the branch whose primary responsibility is the promulgation of the laws of the land. It is not by happenstance that the House Ways and Means Committee called its version of the 1988 trade bill "the most comprehensive restructuring of basic U.S. trade policy since the Trade Act of 1974" and declared that the bill would establish a national trade policy.[7]

The pivotal role of Congress—and hence of trade legislation—means that trade policy is conducted in cycles that begin and end in legislative action. At the start Congress uses the delegating legislation to wind the clock by signaling the direction it wants U.S. trade policy to take and delineating the authority it is willing to give to the executive.[8] At the end of the process Congress evaluates the results of the policy and decides whether to renew the executive's authority and pass implementing legislation.[9] Between the two ends of the cycle is the running clock, the actual conduct of the trade policy by the executive. To bridge the gap between Congress's constitutional responsibility and the inability of "all 535 of us here in the Congress to negotiate trade agreements with the rest of the world,"[10] Congress and the executive have established institutions that reinforce the mutual dependence.

The Real Constitutional Debate over Commerce

In providing for formal congressional supremacy in trade, the framers of the Constitution did not have in mind the resolution of the modern constitutional debate. Their chief concern was not to decide how to divide the federal authority over trade between the president and Congress; rather the Constitutional Convention

> was denying powers to the States. . . . In the end and overall, Congress clearly came first, in the longest article, expressly conferring many, important powers; the Executive came second, principally as executive-agent of Congressional policy. Every grant to the President, including those relating to foreign affairs, was in effect a derogation from Congressional power, eked out slowly, reluctantly, and not without limitations and safeguards.[11]

That the Constitution was a response to the exigencies of the time is especially true in the area of foreign trade and commerce. Under the Articles of Confederation, Congress lacked the authority to regulate national commerce and to negotiate commercial treaties. The power to regulate commerce remained in the hands of the individual states. The initial unwillingness to give a national congress authority over commerce was a reaction to

> Britain's attempts to wrest political power from the colonial assemblies in the name of trade regulation. Even after independence had been achieved, there was as much reluctance to entrust the commercial affairs of the individual states to a national entity like the Congress as there had been to acquiesce in the authority of the British Parliament.[12]

Unfortunately, neither the individual states nor the federal Congress could deal effectively with the foreign trade restrictions that plagued the young nation. Once the United States gained independence, the American economy no longer functioned under the protection of the British Empire. On July 2, 1783, the British Privy Council issued an order in council closing the British West Indies to American ships and sailors and barring the entry of all commercially significant American goods into the British West Indies. Farmers, shipbuilders, and merchants, as well as fisherman and whalers, all suffered serious economic dislocations from the loss of the rich triangular trade and the inaccessibility of the important British colonial ports. By 1785 the situation had become so serious that James Madison warned, "In every point of view indeed, the trade of this country is in a deplorable condition."[13]

The initial response of Congress to the commercial restrictions was to send John Adams to Great Britain in 1785 to negotiate a favorable commercial treaty. His mission was handicapped, however, by the fact that Congress lacked the power to regulate national commerce and, therefore, could not retaliate against Great Britain. The British, therefore, did not take Adams's mission seriously, reminding him that Congress did not have the authority to negotiate a commercial treaty.

The response of the individual states was equally ineffective. They were unable to agree on a uniform policy, and their individual efforts at implementing retaliatory legislation against the orders in council collapsed in the absence of such a policy. By 1789 every state but Connecticut had passed laws that imposed special tonnage duties on incoming British ships, levied special taxes on goods imported in British bottoms, or prohibited British vessels from loading American goods in its ports. The inability of all the states to adopt similar measures, however, doomed the discriminatory systems. Connecticut refused to pass any legislation, and the port of New Haven received the British ships that could not land in Massachusetts, New Hampshire, or Rhode Island. Virginia refused to pass discriminatory legislation on the basis that such legislation would be self-defeating if the barred goods could reach Virginia via Maryland and North Carolina. The inconsistency in the application of laws led Massachusetts to suspend its navigation act in July 1786, and Pennsylvania repealed most of its high duties when its neighboring states refused to match the tariff rates.

The inability of either the states or the federal Congress to deal effectively with the commercial crisis was widely recognized at the time. Protest meetings were organized and editorials published in support of a national response to the crisis. By May 1785 one observer noted a consensus among the people in favor of vesting Congress with sufficient powers for the regulation of commerce. By August 1786 one New York newspaper editorialized that the need for federal regulation of trade "has been so often enforced and descanted on that the whole subject appears to be worn threadbare."[14]

Numerous proposals had already been debated in Congress. As early as September 25, 1783, a committee report on the threat posed by the British commercial restrictions urged that a "General Power be somewhere lodged for regulating the concerns of the United States." On April 30, 1784, a new committee recommended that the power to regulate foreign commerce be given to Congress by all the states for fifteen years. One year later another congressional committee under the chairmanship of James Monroe proposed that the ninth article of the Articles of Confederation be amended to permit Congress to exercise control over foreign trade. The highly controversial proposal, which Monroe admitted would create "a deep and radical change in the band of Union," was not acted on. One year later ten states endorsed the recommendation of the fifteen-year grant of commercial power to Congress, three states hesitating because they thought the proposed grant too weak. The proposal was not enacted, however, because the states could not agree on the extent of congressional control. The economic situation of the young nation was progressively worsening, and on August 7, 1786, the grand committee that had been appointed by Congress to consider the question of constitutional reform proposed seven additional articles of confederation, the first being a provision for congressional control of commerce. Again the amendments were not considered.[15]

Both the report of the Annapolis convention of September 1786, which had originally been convened to provide a forum in which state delegations could agree on a uniform trade policy, and the debates in the Constitutional Convention of 1787 reflected the overwhelming consensus on the need to transfer the power for the regulation of commerce from the state to the federal level. According to Madison, federal regulation of commerce, alone among the major changes that the Constitutional Convention recommended, constituted an addition of new powers for Congress, while the other changes constituted an "invigoration" of the original powers of the Union that had been vested in the existing Congress by the Articles of Confederation. Madison explained, however, that while "the regulation of commerce, it is true, is a new power, . . . [it] seems to be an addition which few oppose, and from which no apprehensions are entertained."[16] Madison concluded that the "regulation of foreign commerce . . . had been too fully discussed to need additional proofs . . . of its being properly submitted to the federal administration."[17]

At no time during this period did the modern constitutional issue arise: it was assumed that the new federal role in trade rested in Congress. The question of executive power in foreign trade was not raised. In fact, Alexander Hamilton, in contrasting the limited authority of the new president to that of the king of Great Britain, used congressional power over trade to defend the new presidency: "The one [president of the United States] can prescribe no rules concerning the commerce or currency of the nation; the other [king of Great Britain] is in several respects the arbiter of commerce, and in this capacity can . . . lay embargoes for a limited time."[18]

Trade Policy as Tariff Policy, 1789–1962

From the first tariff act of 1789 until the Smoot-Hawley Tariff Act of 1930, U.S. trade policy consisted primarily of congressional decisions to raise and lower tariffs or to impose and suspend embargoes as the external situation warranted. If the original intent of the framers of the Constitution was to give the power to regulate foreign commerce solely to Congress, the reality of governing under the new Constitution quickly brought the executive branch into the trade arena. In the spring of 1794 Congress, faced with an impending summer recess, authorized the president to place and revoke embargoes "whenever he felt the safety so required." In 1798 the president was empowered to lift, while Congress was not in session, the suspension of the commercial relations with France that Congress had imposed, whenever he was "well ascertained" that French hostilities against America had ended. Congress was faced with similar decisions before adjourning in 1806 and 1809 and opted to give the executive discretion, respectively, to restrict the importation of certain goods and to suspend an embargo.

Congress did not limit the delegation of its commercial authority to periods when it was not in session. In 1799 the discretion that Congress had given the president to discontinue trade restrictions against France lasted over a year and covered congressional sessions that framed the summer recess.[19] In 1824 Congress authorized the president to suspend discriminatory duties against a number of European countries whenever the foreign country had made reciprocal exemptions. Presidents from John Quincy Adams to Rutherford B. Hayes used this authority to issue tariff adjustment proclamations.[20]

From 1789 to 1930 Congress enacted nine major revisions of the U.S. tariff schedule. In doing so, Congress viewed itself as dealing primarily with domestic questions of raising revenue, in the early days of the nation, and, more generally, of protecting U.S. industry. Although these tariff acts gave successive presidents the authority to adjust tariffs, the authority was carefully circumscribed, and it was Congress, for all intents and purposes, that set the tariffs. For example, the Fordney-McCumber Tariff Act of 1922, while giving the president the authority to adjust duty rates by as much as 50 percent to equalize production costs between the United States and competing countries, brought tariff rates to record levels. Presidents Warren G. Harding, Calvin Coolidge, and Herbert Hoover used the authority sparingly, adjusting tariffs (with the exception of five items, upward) on only thirty-eight items of the thousands of tariff lines on the U.S. schedule. The Smoot-Hawley Tariff Act included specific tariff schedules for more than 20,000 products and set U.S. tariffs at an all-time high.

"The worst tariff bill in the nation's history," as Senator Robert La Follette of Wisconsin called Smoot-Hawley, ended the period of intensive congressional involvement in tariff setting.[21] With the passage of the Reciprocal Trade Agreements Act of 1934, Congress went out of the tariff-setting business and delegated authority to the president to negotiate bilateral, reciprocal trade agreements.[22] The president was given the authority for three years to reduce tariffs by as much as 50 percent of the 1934 rate. The three-year negotiating authority was renewed in 1937 and 1940 and, for two years, in 1943. By 1945 the United States had negotiated twenty-eight reciprocal trade agreements and had used up all the original negotiating authority contained in the 1934 act. The 1945 trade act gave the president three-year authority to reduce tariffs by 50 percent of the 1945 rate. Under this authority the United States entered into the first round of multilateral trade negotiations under the General Agreement on Tariffs and Trade (GATT), in which tariffs were reduced on more than 45,000 products that accounted for more than half of world trade.[23] Between 1945 and 1962 Congress granted the president limited new tariff-negotiating authority and for relatively short periods of time. This still permitted the United States to participate in five rounds of multilateral trade negotiations. The Trade Expansion Act of 1962, which provided the authority for the Kennedy round of multilateral trade negotiations (1962–1967), was the last of such trade bills that focused primarily on tariffs.

As long as trade policy was tariff-setting policy, congressional power to regulate commerce could easily be adapted to the reality of international economic relations. Congress could either enact laws that set the tariff rates, as it generally did through the 1930 tariff act, or delegate tariff-setting authority to the president, as it did from 1934 through the Trade Expansion Act of 1962. In either case Congress was able to exercise its control over the process. In delegating its tariff-setting authority, Congress could put a time period on the delegation, limit the depth of the cuts, and instruct the president, if it wanted, to exclude certain categories of products from the negotiations. In particular, the expiration date on the negotiating authority allowed Congress to assess how the executive branch had used the authority that Congress had given it.[24]

Today's Trade Policy Cycle

As a result of the deep and broad tariff cuts negotiated in the Kennedy round, tariffs ceased to be the major barrier to international trade. The shift in the focus of subsequent negotiations to nontariff barriers to trade (NTBs) seriously challenged Congress's continued ability to control the process.[25] No longer could Congress have a clear idea when it delegated its authority to the president what the final package would look like. Many of the NTBs were statutorily based, and any changes in the measures that would be negotiated as part of a multilateral round would require subsequent implementing legislation. The first U.S. attempt to negotiate a reduction in NTBs failed, because Congress refused in 1967 to pass the necessary legislation to implement two agreements (an antidumping code and a revision of the American selling price system of customs valuation) that the executive had negotiated, without advance authority, during the Kennedy round. This congressional rejection had a profound impact on both Congress and the executive when they next considered trade-negotiating authority in 1972. A way had to be found to preserve Congress's clearly defined role, not only in regulating the foreign commerce of the United States but also in enacting the nation's domestic legislation, while giving the president the discretion that he needed to negotiate the elimination of U.S. trade barriers in exchange for similar reductions abroad. Without some advance indication that Congress would pass the required implementing legislation, trading partners would be reluctant to negotiate NTB agreements with the United States.

For the first time in the modern history of the United States, the "democratic dilemma" had confronted those concerned with trade policy.[26] The ability of the United States to adapt the constitutionally mandated congressional supremacy in trade to the requirements of international trade negotiations in the modern era was called into question. The institutions and processes developed since 1972 by Congress and the executive, while new in form, preserve the relative responsibilities of each branch and, as a result, have their antecedents in the 200-year history of how trade policy has been conducted in the United States. Today the authority to conduct trade policy still begins and ends in Congress and is delegated to the president through the legislative process.

The Takeoff. For the second time since the end of the Kennedy round of trade negotiations in 1967, the United States has completed the first phase of the trade policy cycle. The Omnibus Trade and Competitiveness Act of 1988 provides, as did the Trade Reform Act of 1974, the agreed upon rules of the game for the conduct of U.S. trade policy. In both instances Congress delegated authority to the executive, directed the substance of U.S. trade and trade-related policy, and developed and further refined a system to tie its final legislative role to its initial legislative activities in order to ensure a role for itself during the conduct of trade policy.[27]

Both bills gave the president authority to negotiate reductions in tariffs and NTBs both bilaterally and multilaterally for five-year periods. The extent and time limits of the negotiating authorities were the subject of much give-and-take within Congress and between Congress and the executive. In addition, both trade bills contained changes in the administration of U.S. laws that affected the president's flexibility in implementing the laws. Although these laws form part of U.S. trade policy, the debates were essentially over U.S. domestic law and its implementation by the president—not on foreign policy.[28]

Members of Congress did, however, refer to the generic constitutional issue of how much authority Congress should cede to the executive in such foreign policy areas as multilateral and bilateral trade negotiations. Reference to the delegation issue did not, however, introduce a grand constitutional debate; rather, it was used to reinforce the positions of members on the substance of the trade policy. Those members of Congress who supported the trade policy contained in the legislation thought the legislation's delegation of authority proper, while those who opposed the bill's policy contents raised a hue and cry about the constitutional division of labor. It is hard to find any instance during the consideration of either bill when a member of Congress rose and supported the substance of the policy but opposed the improper delegation of authority.

In bringing the 1988 trade bill to the Senate floor, Senator Bentsen defended his committee's bill by interspersing substance with process: "This legislation does not usurp presidential privilege or seize power that does not belong to the Congress. It is certainly not protectionist. But it does recognize that Congress has a constitutional role in the formation of trade policy, and it demonstrates that Congress is prepared to meet its responsibilities."[29] Similarly, Representative Al Ullman, acting chairman of the House Ways and Means Committee during House consideration of the 1974 trade act, reinforced his support for the substance of the bill by declaring that the bill was "the most innovative approach to establishing a real partnership in the conduct of our international trade relations that has ever been proposed."[30]

Opponents of the trade policy have generally been more shrill about the misallocation of authority. Senator Vance Hartke, coauthor of the highly protectionist Foreign Trade and Investment Act of 1971,[31] argued extensively, as would be expected, against the substantive provisions of the 1974 trade act and added, "this [the bill] is the greatest delegation of constitutional authority ever given the President of the United States."[32] Representative Bertram Podell of New York not only opposed the 1974 bill on the grounds that it did not address the U.S. unemployment situation but also questioned whether, in the midst of the Watergate crisis, Congress should grant sweeping new powers to the president "at a time when the present occupant of that high office has abused and usurped powers on a level unparalleled in our history."[33]

The strongest indictment that a member of Congress can make is equating the delegation of authority to either the Gulf of Tonkin Resolution or the War Powers Resolution. Representative James A. Burke of Massachusetts, coauthor with Hartke of the Foreign Trade and Investment Act, opposed the 1974 trade bill on the grounds that it would erode the U.S. economic base and went on to call the bill a "blank check in foreign trade to the President" and a "virtual abdication of congressional authority and interest in the foreign trade area." He reminded his colleagues that to mention "the Gulf of Tonkin is to mention the most flagrant example of congressional abdication of authority" and, as a *coup de grâce*, suggested that the bill be relabeled the trade power transfer act.[34]

Senator Steve Symms of Idaho used similar language when he expressed concern about both the "statist" policies contained in the Senate's version of the 1988 trade bill and the bill's limitations on the president's ability to conduct international trade policy. Calling the real issue a basic power struggle between the president and Congress, he expressed his hope that if trade legislation did pass the Senate and the House it would not be a "trade war power act" that would restrict any administration from operating an effective trade policy.[35]

In addition to delegating authority to the president to conduct policy, both bills contained extensive provisions that set the direction of U.S. trade policy. The 1988 trade bill, for example, contained three overall and seventeen principal negotiating objectives and included, among its 1,000 pages, provisions on the protection of intellectual property rights, telecommunications trade, export enhancement, export controls, and agricultural trade.

For some members of Congress, providing direction to U.S. trade policy is the main purpose of a trade bill. As Representative Don Pease of Ohio remarked, "Congress traditionally uses this occasion to exercise its constitutional prerogative to set the course of U.S. international economic policy. . . . [The 1988 trade bill] is Congress' clearest, most comprehensive statement to date under Article I, Section 8 of the Constitution."[36] Senator Bentsen offered a similar description of the bill: "This trade bill does point America in the right direction. It starts us down the road to achieve these objectives. We cannot achieve those objectives without this bill."[37]

Congress also uses the delegating bills to send messages to our trading partners. The Senate Finance Committee report on the 1988 trade bill pointed out that, whatever the president's constitutional prerogatives in international negotiations, "The President will be a more effective negotiator to the extent he can assure foreign governments that he is implementing a congressional directive, since the Congress is more likely to approve action in accordance with what it has directed than action it had no part in formulating."[38] Senator John Danforth of Missouri wanted the 1988 trade bill to be a signal abroad that "there must be no doubt that Congress and our administration's negotiators agree on fundamental U.S. trade policy objectives and are working in tandem to secure agreements that serve our best interests."[39] Senator John Heinz of Pennsylvania described the bill as reaffirming congressional commitment to the open trading system, "thus significantly enhancing the administration's credibility at the negotiating table."[40]

The problem posed for the conduct of trade policy by the implementation of NTB agreements that involve changes in U.S. law is practical, not constitutional. It does not pit congressional responsibility to regulate commerce under Article I, section 8, of the Constitution against the president's executive power to implement trade policy. Rather, it juxtaposes Congress's responsibility to enact domestic legislation with the president's executive power to negotiate internationally. Without the development of a new process to bridge the two, either the executive's ability to negotiate international NTB agreements would have been severely circumscribed by the uncertainty of eventual congressional approval, or Congress would have become a mere rubber stamp of internationally negotiated changes in U.S. law.

The solution—a fast-track congressional approval procedure for implementing legislation for nontariff agreements—was born out of the desire by the drafters of the Trade Reform Act of 1974 to avoid a replay of Congress's unwillingness in 1967 to consider the two Kennedy round NTB agreements. To deal with the problem, the president first requested authority to implement NTB agreements that involved changes in U.S. law, subject only to a veto by either the Senate or the House. This approach to making domestic law raised serious constitutional questions, and the final bill directed that NTB agreements negotiated in Geneva would not enter into force until Congress had accepted or rejected them under expedited procedures (within sixty days) that precluded legislative amendments.[41] As Representative Martha Griffiths of Michigan said at the time, since "there is no common standard applicable to non-tariff barriers that lends itself to a general delegation of authority as has been done in the case of tariffs . . . the bill . . . provides an answer to this problem of executive authority to negotiate and congressional authority to legislate."[42]

The actual process to implement the fast-track approach was established when the Tokyo round agreements were brought back to Congress in 1979. Since the 1974 trade act precluded floor amendments, the approval process was driven behind closed doors. The Finance and Ways and Means committees drafted "legislation" in closed "non-mark-up sessions" with executive officials present and the trade agreements as the text. These sessions were then followed by a "non-conference" to reconcile the differences between the two committee bills. The "bill" was then sent to the executive branch, which took it under advisement as it developed the final version of the legislation, which it submitted to Congress for its acceptance or rejection.[43] Looking back on that process, Senator Danforth declared in 1987:

> Had implementing legislation come to Congress without fast-track authority, we would have dealt with that legislation in the normal course of events, which meant the full opportunity for delay and for amendment in committee and on the floor, and, therefore, the Congress of the United States could have undone what the negotiators had completed and there would have been no deal at all.[44]

The fast-track authority gives Congress a reasonable opportunity to approve agreements negotiated by the executive. The requirement that Congress have final approval of the internationally negotiated agreements serves the same function for NTBs that the time limitations on tariff-cutting authority serve for tariffs. Both remind the executive of the eventual congressional role not only in implementing the results of the negotiations but also in renewing authority for further negotiations. Notwithstanding the success of this linkage in the case of the Tokyo round agreements and the United States–Canada and United States–Israel free trade area agreements, the 1988 trade bill went two steps further in reminding the president where the final act was to be played.

While Congress extended the NTB agreement negotiating authority for five years, until May 31, 1993, it extended the fast-track approval procedure only until May 31, 1991. It provided, however, for an extension of the fast-track procedure until May 31, 1993, unless either House passes a disapproval resolution before May 31, 1991, because the negotiations are making insufficient progress or an extension is not requested. As a precondition to the extension, both the president and the private sector Advisory Committee for Trade Negotiations (ACTN) will have to submit progress reports on the negotiations ninety days before May 31, 1991. In addition, the bill provides for termination of the fast-track approval process ("reverse fast track") if the Senate Finance and House Ways and Means and Rules committees and both the House and Senate separately pass disapproval resolutions under the fast track within any sixty-day legislative period because the U.S. trade representative (USTR) has failed or refused to consult with Congress on trade negotiations and trade agreements.

The recent internationalization of the U.S. market and the growing importance of trade to our political relations with other countries have prompted Congress to use delegating legislation to legislate solutions to a widening range of international economic issues that were formerly the preserve of the executive branch. In defining its positions on these new issues, Congress has sought to give direction to the executive branch on the content and conduct of U.S. trade-related policy, similar to the delegation of authority that it provides for the conduct of trade negotiations. The inclusion in the 1988 trade bill of provisions on the regulation of foreign investment in the United States, on the punishment of Japan's Toshiba Machine Company and Norway's Kongsberg Trading Company for diverting sensitive machinery to the Soviet Union, and on the formulation of U.S. exchange rate policy, for example, brought Congress into the gray area of the executive-legislative relationship. These issues, while trade-related, also affected vital foreign policy objectives of the United States that were not amenable to the kind of direction Congress had grown accustomed to giving the president on trade negotiations. Because Congress was moving into uncharted waters, the debates, while principally substantive, included such constitutional issues as the proper separation of power between the two branches of government. The administration's objections to the original Senate language, which would have required international exchange rate negotiations, were substantive but included the additional view that "mandatory negotiations intrude upon the President's exercise of foreign affairs powers committed to him by Article II of the Constitution."[45] The debates on these issues were sharp and divisive.[46] Nevertheless, compromises were worked out that permitted Congress not only to go on record with legislative solutions to these problems but to do so in ways that gave the executive branch its needed freedom to conduct U.S. policy on issues that lay at the intersection of trade and foreign policy.

The Conduct of Trade Policy. The executive's need to return eventually to Congress for implementing legislation or renewal of negotiating authority has given Congress the ability to interject itself into the implementation of trade policy. As Senator William Roth of Delaware has pointed out: "The chief executive and the negotiators realize that there is that power in the Congress, and that it must be taken into account by the Administration while it is negotiating trade agreements."[47] This phase of the cycle is essentially controlled by the executive branch, and, to a large extent, Congress can only kibitz the activities of the executive. This role approximates the traditional oversight responsibilities of Congress to investigate and evaluate the executive branch's substantive and procedural performance.[48]

In trade policy Congress's general kibitzing function has become institutionalized to reflect the shared responsibility of the two branches under the umbrella of congressional supremacy. The 1974 trade bill provided that the president pro tempore of the Senate, on the recommendation of the Finance Committee chairman, appoint five senators and the Speaker of the House, on the recommendation of the Ways and Means Committee chairman, appoint five House members to be official advisers to the U.S. delegations to the negotiations with full access to those negotiations. It also provided for full participation in the negotiations of appropriate congressional staffs to keep the committees informed.

The 1988 trade bill further ties the executive's policy implementation to congressional oversight. The bill widens the role of congressional advisers and requires the executive to provide numerous reports to Congress and consult with it not only on the development of past trade policy but also on future trade policy and legislation. The bill also strengthens the private sector advisory system.

The advice of the ten congressional advisers is no longer limited to the negotiations; they are now advisers on trade policy and negotiations and provide advice on the "development of trade policy and priorities for the implementation thereof," in addition to being accredited as official advisers to the U.S. delegations. The USTR is also required to keep these and any other designated congressional advisers and their staffs currently informed on matters affecting U.S. trade policy and "with respect to possible agreements, negotiating objectives, the status of the negotiations in progress, and the nature of any change in domestic law or its administration" that will be required to carry out the trade agreement. Furthermore, the USTR is required to consult on a continuing basis with the Ways and Means, Finance, and any other appropriate committees on "the development, implementation, and administration of over-all trade policy of the United States."

The trade bill also requires the executive to report to Congress on the general course of trade policy. In addition to the report that the USTR must file to get the fast-track authority extended, the executive branch must file the following reports:

- an annual report on the operation of the trade agreements program during the preceding calendar year, which must include information on eleven specific areas of trade policy
- an annual national trade policy agenda, which will provide the outlines and objectives for the coming year's trade policy
- an annual trade projection report, to be jointly prepared and submitted by the USTR and the secretary of the Treasury, so that Congress can "be informed of the impact of foreign trade barriers and macroeconomic factors on the balance of trade of the United States"[49]

Consultations with the appropriate committees on these reports is also called for by the 1988 trade bill.

Private sector involvement in the negotiating process provides another avenue for Congress to keep watch on the course of the negotiations. It is to Congress that the private sector flocks when it is dissatisfied with the progress of the trade negotiations. Congress cannot formally help the private sector during the negotiations, and it is too late for Congress to change the negotiated result at the time it considers the implementing legislation. Private sector support for the negotiations, as a result of involvement in the process, not only facilitates Congress's oversight responsibilities but also ensures public support for the resultant package.

It is therefore not surprising that the requirement in the 1974 trade bill that the executive receive the advice of the private sector was inserted at the insistence of Congress. As a result, an elaborate system of advisory groups, with representatives of labor, industry, agriculture, consumer groups, and the general public, was established to provide advice and information to the negotiators on a formal and continuing basis. The trade bill directed the executive branch to consult formally with these groups regarding "negotiating objectives and bargaining positions before entering into a trade agreement."

The 1988 trade bill broadens the mandate of these groups to include advice on overall trade policy as well as on trade negotiations and requires the executive to seek the private sector's advice before beginning any negotiations and before entering into any trade agreement.[50] Furthermore, the ACTN has its previously mentioned role in the extension of the fast-track procedure.

In establishing the advisory group system, Congress did not intend to exclude the public from its customary role in the formulation of policy. The public still testifies at legislative and oversight hearings on trade matters, and representatives of interest groups continue to lobby both the executive and the legislative branches. This public involvement is, however, unstructured, and the Congress and the executive branch established the advisory group system as a formal mechanism for communicating the broad and sometimes divergent trade interests of the U.S. public to the trade policy makers. With over 800 representatives of the private sector participating in the program, the government receives advice on all aspects of trade policy: from the broad strokes of policy to the specific and technical details of how trade policy affects individual sectors of the U.S. economy.[51]

The Landing. The institutions that were established to bridge the gap between the executive negotiator and the congressional legislator give the latter the ability to influence the outcome when it still matters: during the actual negotiations. Assuming that congressional views are sufficiently taken into account, both parties are then joined during the landing. The focus of the congressional review process is, once again, on the substance of the agreements and whether the original intent of Congress has been carried out. During the debates on the Trade Agreements Act of 1979, which implemented the Tokyo round NTB agreements, a consensus emerged that the intent of Congress, as reflected in the 1974 Trade Reform Act, had been carried out. Senator Gaylord Nelson of Wisconsin, while voting against the 1979 bill because of U.S. concessions on dairy products, affirmed that "the trade pact has met the goal, established by Congress in the 1974 Trade Reform Act, of reducing and, where possible, eliminating tariff and non-tariff barriers to international trade."[52] Representative Charles Vanik of Ohio, chairman of the House Ways and Means trade subcommittee, also referred to the agreements that were brought back from Geneva as a "normal extension of what we did in 1974."[53]

Member after member related the success of the venture to the close executive-legislative cooperation, which signaled the advent of a new era in the trade agreements program. "The Trade Agreements Act," said Senator Abraham Ribicoff of Connecticut, chairman of the Senate Finance subcommittee on international trade, "is the product of a unique and successful constitutional experiment in coordination between the executive and legislative branches before, during, and after an international negotiation."[54] Representative Vanik linked the success of the fast-track process to four factors, two of which were "the willingness of the Executive to consult with the Congress and the private sector, and cooperation between the executive branch and the Congress."[55]

Notwithstanding the euphoria generated by the bill, Congress did not relinquish its authority on the implementation of trade policy. It did not accede to the president's request to renew his basic tariff negotiating and proclamation authority, which, without renewal, was to expire on January 2, 1980. Senator Roth reflected congressional sentiment that ceding tariff-cutting authority is too open-ended unless it is "closely reviewed and discussed with the administration before it is granted." He urged the executive to submit a proposal to Congress when it had "ascertained the need for such authority."[56] Extension of the fast-track authority for NTB agreements, however, did not constitute such an open-ended commitment by Congress, since Congress had final control over the domestic implementation of any NTB agreements. Consequently, that authority was renewed for eight years.

With the passage of the Trade Agreements Act of 1979, a trade policy cycle had come to an end. In the 1974 trade act Congress had set the direction of policy and delineated the authority that it was delegating to the executive, just as it had done in previous trade acts since the founding of the Republic. In the 1979 Trade Agreements Act, Congress had reviewed the results, endorsed them by passing the necessary implementing legislation, and then made a judgment on whether it wanted to start the cycle over again, just as it had done previously.[57]

The Constitutional Consensus on Trade Policy

In his seminal work on foreign affairs and the Constitution, Louis Henkin writes:

> Many of the differences between Congress and the President are not of constitutional dimension, even when the Constitution is invoked in ritual incantation. If [for example] the President vetoes a tariff adopted by Congress, . . . the controversy may be bitter but it does not involve competition for constitutional power—only the kind of conflict prescribed by the Constitution when it separated powers and subdivided functions.[58]

This observation is especially appropriate in the area of trade policy. While much of the rhetoric of the debate may be couched in constitutional terms, it is not about constitutional power. It cannot be, because the Constitution is clear about the constitutional prerogative of Congress in regulating the foreign commerce of the United States. More important, all rhetoric to the contrary, the supremacy of Congress on trade is recognized by all parties in the debate. This shared recognition does not mean that the competition between the branches for control over the direction of U.S. trade policy has not taken place in the course of our history or that it will not continue. It does mean, however, that the competition is not over constitutional issues.

The best evidence of the nonconstitutional nature of the competition is that over the course of the past 200 years the trade policy process has evolved and developed a system and a set of institutions to regulate the competition. The congressional delegation of limited and circumscribed authority to the executive and the subsequent review of the results permit Congress to maintain its control over the conduct and hence over the substance of trade policy. The limited delegations of Congress's trade authority in the early days of the Republic, the reciprocal trade agreements program of the 1930s, the development of the fast-track approval process, and the ability of Congress and the executive branch to reach compromises on legislative initiatives on the politically charged trade-related issues contained in the 1988 trade bill demonstrate that the system of congressional supremacy is adaptable to changing conditions.

Because Congress's primary tool for controlling the executive is legislative, the process may appear to lack clarity. As opposed to an executive branch whose authority emanates from one president, the involvement of 535 legislators and the horse trading associated with passing the legislation that delineates and reviews the policy raise concerns that the resultant trade policy is not coherent and may be misguided. These concerns may grow as Congress increasingly feels pressured to legislate solutions to trade-related issues that affect other components of U.S. foreign policy. Such concerns about the roles of the two branches are substantive and are part of the competition envisioned by the Constitution. The concerns are, however, not constitutional.

5
The Problem of Practice—Foreign Policy and the Constitution

Mark Blitz

In this chapter I discuss the everyday politics involved in making and executing American foreign policy from a constitutional perspective. These days the conduct of these politics, or what we call in our bureaucratic and academic pomposity the foreign policy "process," is almost universally lamented. As occurs with so many lamentations, the separate voices have different cries, but the overall effect is a penetrating wail. For some, Congress is too intrusive; for others it is not intrusive enough. For some, the administration is too ideologically inflexible; for others it is too reactively pragmatic. For some, the departments that conduct foreign policy are too narrowly self-interested and uncoordinated; for others they fail to defend their legitimate independence adequately. The result, so one hears, is fragmented policy that lacks cohesion, direction, and intelligence.

In contrast, I believe that when we properly understand everyday political activity, we will see that it results in and helps secure the consistency and substance appropriate in a liberal democracy's conduct of foreign affairs. In the discussion that follows, I give practical examples of political activity in foreign affairs and reach the preliminary conclusion that there is more cohesion than we think. Then I bring to light more directly the immediate practical and constitutional context for conducting affairs, after briefly pointing out why it is so difficult to observe these affairs commonsensically. Finally, I will use this political perspective to elaborate a more reflective sense of how our constitutionally grounded institutions actually work, and are intended to work, in policy making and execution. This, in turn, will complicate but ultimately confirm the preliminary judgment that our political process yields policy that is basically consistent and intelligent.

Political Activity in Foreign Affairs

In June 1985, the Senate voted to repeal the Clark amendment of 1974 whose effect had been to prohibit the government from aiding Angolan rebels. The administration had not requested the repeal, no testimony about it had been offered in the Foreign Relations Committee, and debate was confined to ten minutes on the Senate floor. The House did not discuss the issues at all, accepting the Senate's action in a conference report whose substance, although guided broadly by the committee chairmen, was determined by negotiations left exclusively to staff.

Throughout 1985, to take a different example, attempts were made to derail the president's decision that international communications satellite systems separate from Intelsat are in the national interest. The effect of the president's decision was to permit competition with Intelsat's global monopoly. Intelstat hired lobbyists to invent strategies to overturn or neuter the decision and to pursue these strategies with all the vigor, sincerity, and casuistry that they could muster. Many were chosen because of political or personal friendship with those they were lobbying, or their staffs. Most were attorneys, who approached their work in a manner indistinguishable from those who lobbied without the protection and pretension of practicing law.

On the other side were not merely the private firms that wished to launch the new satellites but also the Federal Communications Commission, the Commerce Department's National Telecommunications Information Administration, and the State Department's Bureau of International Telecommunications. Their unity had resulted in the president's success in the first place. It was itself hard won and often in danger of self-destruction. At least two of the agencies involved could barely conceal their contempt for each other, and one of them was a congressional invention for which no administration had ever asked.

All groups directed their attention toward four foreign affairs and four more commerce committees, seeking or warding off hearings and legislation by reminding committees of their supposed jurisdictional interests and producing suggestions to implement those interests. They offered and countered technical arguments about transmission capabilities, demographic trends, market conditions, and the like. They invoked multilateral organizations (the International Telecommunications Union), bilateral relations, and the rhetoric of competition and privatization. They stimulated and calmed partisan passions. They maneuvered, dissembled, and pressured. A vague but unmistakable odor of vanity, greed, and ambition enveloped the proceedings.

As a third example, let us consider again the same conference discussions in which the Clark amendment was allowed to disappear but focus now on the heated debate that occurred about Cocom, a group composed of representatives from certain countries and several agencies of the U.S. government that decides what products contain technologies too sensitive to be exported to the Eastern bloc. The conference debate centered on the makeup of the American group and on the relative power of the Defense Department, known to want severe export restrictions, and the State Department, thought to have more moderate views, though less moderate than those of the sales-driven Commerce Department. The disputes about and within Cocom had been media events for the previous year or two, featuring as they did the mixture of money, national security, and gossip about the powerful dear to contemporary writers and readers. The issue was forced by a member of one legislative branch, largely, as best anyone could or would tell, because of personal dislike for a key member of the executive. Staff from the other legislative branch made defense of the executive's position a central goal of the entire conference proceedings, buttressed by the official himself but not by the executive branch as a whole, whose support was nominal. The compromise reached on Cocom clearly favored the official's position but to some degree at the expense of the administration's position on the satellite issue. Staff could not allow the legislator who lost on Cocom to be defeated visibly on a second issue crucial to him, and his stance on international communications satellites differed from the president's.

As a final example, in 1985 years of American concern about our treatment in the United Nations came to a head in the congressional appropriations and authorization process. Amendments in earlier years that restricted funding to the United Nations because of various disgraces in the Middle East were now matched by still more amendments inspired by further Middle Eastern disgraces, by fears of spying under UN cover, and by general contempt for shoddy accounting and gross overspending. These amendments were largely the creature of junior legislators, often working with public policy research groups. None of the amendments had been asked for or supported by the executive branch, although the president's unhappiness with the United Nations was well known. Some, however, were supported by the agencies making up the intelligence community and the congressional committees that oversee them. All were fought by the State Department, but several—those supported by the intelligence community—more vigorously than others. The State Department's own fiscal crisis, however, its need to support its basic operations and to fund massive new physical security measures, let it see the utility of freeing UN funds for its own purposes. Its ardor for the fight was therefore dampened. Various outside groups fought more vigorously, and the UN high command, including the secretary general, pleaded directly with key legislators. They found surprisingly little congressional support. The traditional legislative allies of the United Nations understood the difficulty of their cause. More significant, they very much desired successful legislation and did not want the authorization and appropriations bills stalled. The result was an important change in our financial relations with the United Nations that the administration had not organized and the congressional leadership had not instigated.

The same authorization process from which these four examples have been drawn also permitted the continued operation abroad of hundreds of embassies, consulates, and cultural centers. It supported thousands of hours of radio broadcasting, millions of dollars of academic scholarships, and uncountable trips, visits, conferences, and negotiations. It authorized salaries for the tens of thousands of diplomats, bureaucrats, clerks, and political officials ensconced in the State Department and the United States Information Agency. It permitted land to be rented, buildings to be built, contracts to be let, and all of this to be investigated, audited, evaluated, and researched. Remarkably, however, the vast majority of these broadcasts, scholarships, negotiations, audits, discussions, and diplomatic missions were conducted by the executive with a free hand. Although previously legislated standards guided this activity and the authorizing process implicitly or explicitly reaffirmed these codes, Congress exercised little practical oversight. In the great bulk of detailed business, the executive administered, and still administers, largely unchecked.[1]

Political Activity and Policy Coherence

These examples are meant to recall what all students already know about contemporary American government: that its effort is a complex result of legislative and executive action with both the legislature and the executive separated into sometimes conflicting units, all influenced by public opinion organized through lobbyists and the media. It would have been easy to have selected still more examples to show the influence of the courts, local interests, family, and friends. From such examples, readily multiplied, one can derive the conclusion that the American government is too fragmented to be effective. Indeed, our examples all involve important but relatively minor matters: if the government is a battleground on which is spilled the blood of tele-communications competitors, imagine the complexity when strategic defense, arms control, Central America, and South Africa are at issue. Yet this same set of examples contains instances of far-reaching activity accomplished quickly, easily, silently, and largely unopposed. Perhaps the issue is not so much ineffectiveness as it is incoherence. Yet, over the long term, things seem less incoherent than they do at any given time. The repeal of the Clark amendment fit together with the administration's policy in southern Africa, the limits on UN spending became part of the administration effort to rationalize the United Nations and to diminish its significance simultaneously, and the continuing debate about international telecommunications is a normal expression of financial competition amid changing technology well within the boundaries that might define debilitating confusion.

Indeed, if we consider the more important recent issues, we might also wonder whether ineffectiveness or incoherence is in fact rampant. President Reagan was able to reorient strategic thinking seriously and to achieve massive budget outlays to support his concept, with surprisingly little staff discussion, bureaucratic competition, or congressional opposition. Budget requests for strategic defense have doubtless been cut and several legislative hurdles must be crossed before working systems come into being that will test the practical limits and possibilities of the new strategic concept. Perhaps, indeed, they will never be crossed. Do these hurdles display incoherence and ineffectiveness or, rather, sober caution in the face of remarkable executive energy? Is the issue one of improper congressional meddling or, more simply, one of differences in judgment and vision? Similarly, in Central America, is the structural issue one of unwarranted congressional interference in an executive function or, indeed, of unwarranted executive flouting of legislative authorities? Or, more simply and more profoundly, is it one of different judgment, opinion, and character, opposing views of what the crisis is in the hemisphere and what should be done about it? Even the odd process that buried the Boland amendment would not have been supported in the first place had not many representatives thought it desirable. After all, the same process derided in Central American policy worked coherently and effectively in Afghanistan. Indeed, the same process that led one and all to condemn either the Iran-contra investigations or the events investigated worked quite smoothly to allow the American navy to patrol the Arabian gulf forcefully in 1987 and 1988, and this in the face of battle decisions—the *Stark* and the

Vincennes—that in another atmosphere could easily have led to profound partisan and institutional turmoil.

Political Action and Theoretical Confusion

This suggests that our political struggles give more coherent results than we sometimes think. To assess this claim, we need to understand better the immediate perspective of the participants in the struggle and the direct manner in which this struggle is constitutionally sanctioned.

When a staff aide, assistant secretary, legislative director, or committee chairman confronts a political task, he faces it as a matter that requires political judgment. People think about how to receive an appropriation, deal with the sudden death of an ally, or pass successful tax law. Yet when we discuss American politics reflectively, it is peculiarly difficult to recapture how things look as issues of immediate concern. One reason is that matters of political judgment always face us in an environment that defines the tasks and sets the direction in which they are solved. Today's reflective student, however, can hardly avoid discussing the environment itself: he will talk of the theory of legislative-executive relations, generalize about alliance politics, or rehearse the just distribution of wealth among the rich, the poor, and the middle class. The practical man in America also talks of such things. Sometimes he does so in proportion to uncertainty or failure: if the results he wants are especially hard to obtain, he laments the breakdown of Congress, the unchecked courts, or the imperial presidency. Yet sometimes he does so because theoretical or scientific questions are immediate elements of the issues needing practical decision—military strategy depends upon technology, economic issues upon monetary theory, and "human services," apparently, on theories of dependence. Moreover, the tools and institutions with which we Americans address issues—our ways and means—are themselves products of reflection. The institutional setting through which we make practical judgments is a product of the modern political science of Locke, of Hamilton, of Madison. Indeed, our institutions have spawned a lengthy literature of legal and scholarly analysis and are seen even by the most practical man through a haze of theoretical invention and scholarly disquisition. Moreover, it is sometimes entirely natural that practical men deal with the environment defining immediate issues, rather than with the issues themselves. When practical questions involve rich and poor, free and slave, or friend and foe, it is always possible that discussion of goals and directions will overstep the limits and guidelines set by our political environment. Debate about deeper standards can erupt naturally within some political situations even if there exist hardly any scholars or scientists. The outstanding American example is the political argument leading to our civil war.

It is therefore more difficult than it seems at first to recapture fully the immediate situation for political action, because our situation deals with so much that comes to us from the outside and has been produced theoretically. Nonetheless, we can at least discern several important elements of the way things look within this horizon.

The Immediate Context for Political Action

Within a political situation, one begins by accepting what is given. If there are many agencies engaged in an issue, one deals with them. If Congress is involved, one deals with it. Normally, one neither wishes nor needs more officials and institutions involved than have involved themselves already. But restricting government agencies or Congress and its members is difficult. If an issue at all touches one's legal or bureaucratic competence, one can engage it. Every cabinet department, many noncabinet agencies, most major congressional committees, and the White House itself, for example, have something or other to say about the use of illegal drugs. Indeed, it is remarkable how easy it is to become involved or to break off involvement. Arms control, for instance, is dominated at any given time by the State Department, the Defense Department, the National Security Council, or the president's own office. Within the State Department it can be dominated by the European Bureau, the Political-Military Affairs Bureau, or the secretary. Within the Defense Department, anyone from the International Security Bureau to the service heads can be decisive. Officials in the Department of Energy, the intelligence community, or the U.S. Information Agency could use their toehold to become relevant. In the first term of the Reagan administration, for example, reporters incessantly analyzed the split between the assistant secretary of state for European affairs, who had earlier headed the Bureau of Political-Military Affairs, and the assistant secretary of defense for international security affairs.[2] By the end of the second term, although State's European Bureau was still central, the other two were not. Certain individuals—Paul Nitze for example—have been significant in arms control whatever their bureaucratic perch.

While this is not to say that possibilities for involvement are unbounded or that within the executive they do not all come to a head with the president, involvement in issues cannot easily be controlled. Moreover, inciting congressional committees or executive agencies to action is often a strategy for getting one's own way. Within any agency, for example, bureaucrats constantly bring disputes to a higher level or threaten to do so. Immediate supervisors expend much effort to limit this practice, and distant supervisors expend much effort to permit it. If someone is already in control, however, he has no need to involve others; restricting the competition, thereby attaining policy or administrative monopoly, is everyone's usual wish and, on many small issues, the usual outcome. Ultimately, therefore, everyone both wants and does not want strict hierarchy, limited involvement, and full coordination.

During the first term of the Reagan administration, as one more example, funding and direction of our foreign aid program were controlled by the administration together with the Senate and House appropriations subcommittees. The House and Senate authorizing committees were never able to pass foreign aid and security as-sistance bills. At the beginning of the second term, the authorizing committees, under new leadership, were determined to pass legisla-tion and regain some control. The administration, however, had be-come comfortable dealing only with the appropriations committees. Foreign aid is contentious, is disliked by most citizens, and has become a lightning rod for controversy and special interests. Who needs to manage more than one bill and more than one set of congres-sional committees? The administration, therefore, was cool to the authorizers' new efforts. Nonetheless, once the authorizing commit-tees made clear that they were likely to succeed—that, indeed, they would pass several amendments disapproved by the administration if that was the cost of doing business in their chambers—the administra-tion, which relied on the committees for other support, was forced to work with them. The small circle that for a few years controlled foreign aid had been opened.

In practice, therefore, one begins by taking seriously whoever makes himself a serious factor, even if—precisely if—one wishes that there be as few serious "players" as possible. This is why we so easily conclude that decisions are made exclusively through compromise, bargaining, and splitting of differences. Given the large number of participants, we then further believe that policy usually takes a medi-ocre course and, in fact, an unstable one, because everyone comes away with something even if the final product is in part self-contradic-tory. (In Congress, a shrewd legislator gives everyone some reason to vote for a bill.) Indeed, because this story is repeated with different contestants for different issues, the sum total of policy might seem spectacularly incoherent. Yet, we have seen that nearly single-minded control and action sometimes occur. In fact, I will expand my earlier assertion and claim that wandering as the course of affairs may sometimes appear, both the general direction and the specific goals of American foreign policy have been quite clear since the Second World War and remarkably straightforward in the administration that has just passed.

Constitutional Sanction for Political Struggle

How can a policy that results from so many hands be so consistent? The simplest answer would be that American government is designed to establish such a result, and although such simplicity overlooks many subtleties, it is essentially correct. The method of checks and balances, generally understood as the active form of daily American politics, is as significant in foreign affairs as it is in domestic ones. It is not peculiar that so many are involved in foreign affairs, with so few boundaries set among their authorities and so little cost for overstepping the boundaries that exist. If government is intended to be limited, to represent and not to rule, to let liberty flourish, to abide by equally applied laws, and to rebuke any grounds for permanently unequal privileges, then it is unlikely indeed to concentrate authority. Checks and balances within government are an elegant practical mechanism to prevent such concentration from emerging. Although federalism is the related mechanism, in the conduct of foreign affairs it would obviously be an imperfect check on executive overstepping because it would threaten the country's existence as such.

We have all the more reason, then, for these internal checks when we conduct foreign affairs. Imperial adventurism, after all, is a chief sin of kings and queens. How could one leave our executive unchecked in the area where executive ambition is so insistent? A tyrannical executive is, among other things, one who risks citizens in war for private imperial gain.[3] Among the balances necessary in limited government, therefore, is precisely the balance against the weight of executive presence in foreign and military affairs.

Let us continue to examine the Constitution from the commonsensical point of view. To do so is to be unimpressed with the argument that the executive has "sole" responsibility for foreign affairs. The president is commander in chief, but Congress provides for the common defense, regulates foreign commerce, provides for naturalization, punishes "offenses against the law of nations," declares war, grants letters of marque and reprisal, makes rules concerning capture on land and water, raises an army, and provides for a navy and for a militia to repel invasion. The president makes treaties and appoints ambassadors but only with the Senate's advice and consent—and never free from a judicial power that considers treaties to be law and ambassadors to be subject to the Supreme Court in the cases that affect them. And although it is the president who "receives ambassadors and other public ministers," it is in Congress that all revenue is raised and by Congress that the president can be impeached and tried.

Taken together, all this certainly suggests shared authority in foreign affairs. By specifying the president's authority over the army and his power to receive ambassadors, however, the Constitution clearly intends the president to exercise much direct and immediate control. The Constitution normally says so little about what the president is expected to do that anything so specific stands out. What I have just recalled about Congress, however, makes manifest the legislature's importance as well. In fact, although there is much to lament in the way the contemporary Congress conducts its business—itself receiving (and sending) "ambassadors," for example, with sometimes extraordinary misjudgment—foreign affairs obviously now command so much of the country's resources that Congress's authority must be exercised constantly. The immediate overall impression the Constitution gives, I believe, is that within their joint authority Congress and the president are responsible together for what we today call the long view—confirming appointees, declaring war, funding an army, ratifying treaties—with the president, as commander in chief and head of state, responsible for executing here and now. When the long view is so often overwhelmed by necessity and when all occurs in a press of intense, immediate, expensive detail, though, it is difficult in practice to distinguish one thing from another. Today, the shared authority of the contemporary Congress and the president often seems more significant than does any special presidential responsibility for immediate execution. The president's capacity to deal directly with foreign governments and to make immediate military adjustments shows us that he still has special standing. Our most sudden military and political possibility, however—the launching of strategic nuclear weapons—shows the imprudence of asking a responsible Congress not to meddle in the execution of immediate affairs.

Executive and Legislative Action

We must expand, elucidate, and better integrate these common sense views of the Constitution and of immediate political practice if we are to assess more thoughtfully whether our political process works well in foreign affairs. We can accomplish this by discussing further the meaning of executive and legislative action. This discussion should clarify how the defining element of our politics—the constitutional structures as embodying the founders' intentions—works.

Executive and legislative action begins with the constitutional fact of dual authority. This fact has its impact because everyone knows that sooner or later he must deal with the other branch, the other House, the other department, or the other side. By and large, this realization comes sooner for legislators than for executives, because the executive can normally display the characteristics that define him more visibly in foreign affairs than in other areas. These characteristics cluster around concepts such as leadership, energy, risk, and loyalty. The successful executive takes his bearings less from given situations than from the future as he would like to see it. He is not guided by a here-and-now defined by others and does not conceive his task to be managing what others present him. Rather, he understands the current situation as a novel set of problems and opportunities leading to the future he has projected. Because he is practical, he attends carefully to the immediate constellation of interests and forces but primarily from the perspective of his own plans, not the perspective of others' self-understanding, and he concentrates more on the new constellation of interests and forces that will be shaped by each of his actions. Skillful subordinates are important, but loyalty, friendship, and trust are more decisive than competence.

The successful executive is most at home in an atmosphere of battle, challenge, new beginning, revival, and enterprise, and his characteristic projection of novel possibilities and standpoints leads him to create such an atmosphere even where it is not commonly recognized. Ultimately he seeks for himself an admiration that goes beyond mere respect, and his way of seeing and doing things so persistently from his own viewpoint leads followers and observers to attribute to him outstanding, even uncanny, qualities.

The effective legislator is as political in his thinking and acting as the effective executive. He too considers concrete interests and wishes here and now and thinks about how they can seem to be satisfied by his programs. He too always looks toward what can gain this or that person's support and cajoles or persuades with the tools that work in the given case. He too does not weigh abstract "values" to reach a decision but, rather, considers and strives for his purpose in ways closely tied to the immediate, specific context within which he works. Unlike the successful leader, however, the legislator does not project a possibility in which he sees people and things in a new light. He does not redefine and reorient. Rather, he sees common solutions to commonly defined problems and understands how the new situation, the compromise that he projects, can be made attractive to people in terms of their current self-understanding. Although the executive may also begin from current concerns, one measure of his ability is his capacity to have others come to grasp and articulate their concerns in his new terms. The measure of the legislator's ability, however, is his capacity to bring about a satisfactory result, still in the old terms. Whereas President Reagan finally succeeded in making us at once both conservative and entrepreneurial, his legislative team needed to discover how to pass the tax cut before so many became Reaganites. In general, the legislator's gift is his ability to fashion and effect compromise, while the executive's gift is to construct and lead a striking enterprise. Needless to say, neither executives nor legislators are confined to one branch, and few legislators or executives are completely effective. These general characteristics and their paler imitations, however, help to explain the push and pull of everyday politics. Our next task, therefore, will be to outline more precisely how executive energy and legislative action express and embody the actual operation of checks and balances.

The successful executive would be too dominant were he not opposed by others of his own type. For one thing, the need for and possibility of popular consent would become increasingly remote were everything to become merely an element in some leader's master plan. The legislative body and the legislative character, however, are neither swift nor bold enough to limit executive action properly. In domestic affairs, the executive is limited by state governors and by the lesser executives who direct agencies. More decisively, he is limited by the vast areas still reserved to the private entrepreneur and by the almost incredible distance our politics takes from controlling speech and religion. We trust tolerance rather than censorship to limit possible excesses of speech and religion, however, precisely because tolerance permits the rise of doctrines and doctrinaires who compete and countervail.

We also expect tolerance to work because the interests of our citizens are focused primarily on spiritual expression through material creation and enjoyment. The American executive is trained to take his bearings from the ordinary concerns with which government deals. Crusades against drugs and illiteracy, wars on crime and dependency, missions to save and promote democracy characterize our successful political leaders. Their reshaping, redefining, and reformulating take place within the ambit of the equal protection of practical popular rights. It is just this protection that our founders created our institutions to serve. Precisely because of this horizon, consent of

the governed is both necessary and desirable, and legislative moderation enables discovery of common solutions to commonly discernible
problems that the sum of individual actions cannot ameliorate.

Although executive action is a fact, one might therefore wonder
what good it is. At its best, the constant overstepping by executive
types enables the community to meet threats and seize opportunities
that would otherwise overpower it. The continual reshaping by executives also enables the community to assimilate concerns that
would be pushed aside in ordinary representative politics. Our
greater executives see before others do the need to create friendships,
prepare for battle, and admit new talent, because they see things in an
almost imperial light. Our lesser executives do this to a lesser degree.
Executive energy and pride, therefore, are useful in a world that will
not stand still even when government is meant to be a limited enterprise. They are also desirable for another reason. By accident or
design, every country enhances and perpetuates some set of human
virtues. Our grounding in natural rights leads us to encourage the
self-interest, moderation, prudence, and respect for equality politically visible in legislative compromise. These, however, do not en-
compass human excellence. Executive pride is good because it allows
the expression within our country of a kind of courage, generosity,
practical wisdom, and love of distinction—the kind that can result in
support of liberal democracy.

Of course, such characteristics unchecked make limited government impossible, and this is why our politics checks itself as it does. It
is good, not bad, that a president must sometimes fight his cabinet
and agencies in order to dominate his own policy. In the executive
branch there must be several people of quality if the president is to be
sufficiently tested or resisted; there must also be people of quality if
he is lacking. It is good, not bad, that some in Congress act more as
enterprising executives than as ordinary, or even extraordinary com-
promisers. The legislature as a legislature would be too weak unless
some tried to make it a vehicle swift and strong enough to carry their
own hopes. It is also useful that so many in the executive conduct
themselves merely as special elements within legislatively dominated
activity. They regulate, adjust, ameliorate, enforce, and execute only
within the compromises that enable their practices to be authorized
and funded. Unless this usually happened, legislative compromise
would seldom be successful, and the executive would become too
contentious for the legislature to bear. Yet if everyone in the executive
branch conducts himself this way, there is no genuine executive
energy where it is most necessary and appropriate because executives
and, most obviously, the president can accomplish more individually,

can reshape, reform, and lead more successfully than can anyone who is only part of a legislative body. In turn, the beauty of our legislative branch—that it directs its members to shape and be shaped in consensual compromise—works best when most of its members are not true leaders but, rather, express the distinctive moderation fostered by our regime.

Consistent Purpose in Foreign Affairs

This constitutional basis of the push and pull of our everyday politics, thought through in terms of the characteristically political understanding of our political men, helps make clear why the purpose of our foreign affairs remains quite consistent even though their conduct is so often fragmented. The horizon of our justified political activity is the set of concerns salient to men and women all of whom we believe to be endowed equally with natural rights to life, liberty, and the pursuit of happiness. Our country conspires to make the love of distinction serve this love of equality, and our most distinctive citizens know this and approve this, most of all.[4] The national wealth we defend from outsiders, for example, is understood by almost all to be good and to be a good aided by the free flow of property and ideas. Some ask for a level playing field, but who in good conscience asks for one tilted in our direction? Some worry about ethnic imbalance and insularity, but how many publicly seek to keep the talented from our shores merely because they are not yet natives? The national independence we defend is understood by everyone to be desirable and since the Second World War to require neither expansion nor contraction. Some desire more weapons and some fewer, but who denies the need to be secure and to support the technology necessary for security? Some wish our allies would contribute more to defense, and some are already satisfied, but who does not tie our own independence securely to allies? And who would wish to be defeated by or to become identical to our enemies? The appropriateness of preferring for other countries the liberal institutions that defend rights is now broadly visible. Some worry more about careful treatment of our nondemocratic allies; some worry less. But who does not believe that these alliances will be secured better when all become democrats? Some believe that we must intervene when likely democrats are engaged in civil war; some do not. But who prefers that the oligarch or tyrant wins? The basic direction of our foreign politics is clear and widely agreed to: our differences seem large only if we know little.

These differences, of course, are nonetheless quite real at the time they occur, and they are the material of everyday politics. Disagreements sometimes open into debate that brings to the fore profound questions, but our constitutional structures work to close these openings and to narrow discussion so that it is only a mechanism within legislative and executive interplay. The opportunities this interplay affords lead to the apparent confusion of which I gave examples earlier. This confusion, though, is a result of the way in which America keeps within its limits. The struggle of interests to find their common ground in compromise, and of leaders to make their name, usually results in a reasonably steady and self-assured course.

This consensus is why most foreign policy debates involve implementation rather than design, and it is why discussions of the proper role for this or that bureaucratic agency are so sterile. The director of the Central Intelligence Agency (CIA) and our ambassador to the United Nations have at various times enjoyed nominal or effective cabinet status. After his election, President-elect Bush was reported to believe that these positions should once more belong to implementers, not policy makers.[5] He effected his wish simply by choosing heads and subheads who carry themselves more as regulators and administrators than as true executives.

The CIA is also a useful example to help us weigh the common view that the clash of agencies is merely a battle of their interests, narrowly defined, with eventual resolution at the most ordinary level. In opposition, I would argue that the years of controversy about the CIA have not been caused by an agency secure in pursuing its bureaucratic interest. Its conventional interest is to be quietly valuable, content with gathering information, and doing more only if it is noncontroversial. When, however, its director takes a stand on ground from which others shrink, maneuvering and manipulating to accomplish what others no longer want accomplished, conceiving his agency's proper tasks as others no longer conceive them, he, in fact, puts his agency deeply at risk. With good luck and a steady hand, however, he also allows it to prosper eventually in its expanded functions or lost functions newly asserted. In the broadest sense, therefore, one cannot say simply either that pursuing or shrinking from risky covert actions is in the CIA's interest or that its actions stem largely from what its leaders perceive their interests to be. It all depends on how bold the director or other leaders have been in staking the claim to conduct these actions, how thoughtful they have been in pursuing them, how generous they have been in giving less gifted subordinates the means to continue to carry them out, and how fair they have been in sharing responsibility and taking guidance so that they are useful for the country. When the executive succeeds in all this, the functions his agency serves become part of a new, broad set of interests that future bureaucrats defend. Others in government proceed to applaud his vision, and the country believes it has been well served. When he fails, those who defend the old narrow interests sagely nod their heads. Others in government proceed to condemn his overreaching, and the country believes it has been harmed. Indeed, the country has been harmed if it has lost a capacity for action that no one else in government is aggressive enough to seize.

Even unimaginative agency heads will need some of the executive's pride in order to succeed, because the loyalty of the most able subordinates can be commanded only when the executive positions his agency at or near the top of something. For this reason, most successful executives pursue more than the immediate interests of their agency. This sometimes leads them to clash with their more ordinary staff. After all, the immediate self-interest of most bureaucrats is to live undisturbed. Few grasp that for them to exist comfortably, their leaders must gamble a bit, in order to show that their agencies can be useful in the new situations that inevitably arise. Only in this way can they safely hold on to what they already have. In fact, an agency head who always accommodated would deprive the country of whatever talents or insights his agency commanded. The political process ignores those who do not care and soon redistributes their resources. The clash of agencies is therefore more often resolved either by a compromise that reaches beyond the immediate interest of bureaucrats or by the triumph of the most aggressive leader than it is by the simple splitting of immediate differences.

Because this process of executive enterprise and legislative compromise is how government is at once limited and effective, few set constraints enable us to define properly the role of this or that agency or even of the legislative or the executive branch. It is reasonable, for example, for Congress to assert constant control over intelligence agencies precisely because their scope is so undefined. But the president will always make the key choice about the actual range of any intelligence agency by nominating a head who fits his idea of the amount of entrepreneurial freedom—the "policy role"—that the agency should have.

This shared appointment and confirmation power, moreover, makes clear that lesser executives, however aggressive they are, are subordinate to both the president and the Congress; the president's exclusive dismissal power makes clear that they are subordinate to the president first of all; and the restraints of authorization and appropriation further help keep activities within constitutional purposes. The action of even the most aggressive subordinate official is therefore constrained. Still, an astounding amount of territory is open to executives. The transportation secretary is not the secretary of state or of health and human services. But his control of aviation and the Coast Guard can make him decisive in dealing with terrorism and drugs. Nonetheless, the formal constraints of appointment and appropriation increase the costs to any subordinate officer of extreme overreaching. They keep him somewhat in check and make it more practical for him to focus instead on the presidency. Here immodesty may reappear, however, for it is difficult to attain this prize without achieving a reputation for something outstanding—the "Massachusetts Miracle" or extraordinarily loyal captaincy in the "Reagan Revolution" to take the election of 1988—that steps beyond tasks ordinarily conceived. Able subordinate executives, and not merely legislators, are therefore a threat to any presidency. Their ambition, however, is significant in keeping him in line and ultimately keeping his policy within limits. Still, governmentally, only a president can attempt to pursue successfully his own broad design, to see and manipulate in his own terms, because only he can take for granted sufficient scope and authority. Everyone else begins by taking him more seriously than he takes them.

Presidents, of course, are only fitfully successful executives, and most are mere administrators with broad functions. In any case, they are checked by the press of legislative interests and by competition from other leaders public and private: the singular power of the president must be earned and earned again. He does start ahead of the others, though, and enjoys the further advantage that it is natural for the country to be addressed as one, and the president most obviously stands for this one. Not only does he command the army, but he is the head of state. Indeed, it is as head of state that he can so easily use his other authorities to take for granted an immense place in foreign affairs—he is expected, as one, to represent the whole. This is why his preeminence in foreign affairs seems sensible even when we acknowledge shared congressional authority.

This immediate preeminence of the president is also more acceptable in foreign affairs than it would be in domestic affairs because the clash of constituent interests that justifies domestic legislation is less great, and without the fig leaf of constituent interests we more easily see legislative action as partisanship or individual ambition. Securing national wealth against foreign interests can of course bring out a split among domestic economic interests, but the basic distribution—for our citizens, not theirs—is clear. Securing national independence can involve disputes over regional economic interests, but every region in the country wants the president to command forces sufficient to defend it. Calm pursuit of our national security can be overwhelmed

by disputes about the range and content of the liberties we should
secure for ourselves and others, but for almost all every regime except
liberal democracy is illegitimate. The president's natural executive
singularity is thus supported in foreign affairs by considerable unity.
This supremacy, moreover, makes the kind of clashes we expect in
domestic affairs seem surprising and unjustified in foreign affairs. It
also leads legislative officials to be especially deferential to the president when he summons them to discuss emergencies. To begin with,
all they ask is to be "consulted," not merely informed. They do not
demand to lead. This is only to say, however, that the president has
and should have an advantage. For the substance of everyday politics,
the clash among executive ambitions and between executive enterprise and legislative compromise is necessary if our foreign affairs are
to be conducted in a manner appropriate to representative government and are not to suffer from the misplaced secrecy, arbitrariness,
nepotism, and vainglory that can characterize executive dominance.

Conclusion

The picture I have drawn is in many ways too sanguine. Too much
today is seen by political men in the artificial terms of scholarship,
science, and ideology. Too much in education and the media is unchecked and extreme, making it more difficult than it should be for
people to judge their leaders commonsensically on the basis of reputation that can be believed. Too much in technology seems closed to
political understanding. Political men may check each other, but too
little is held beyond the scope of governmental and legal control to
begin with: there is too much with which to contend and too low a
cost for indiscipline in the executive and legislative branches. Were all
this to be explored, however, as it should be, I believe we would still
conclude that we are well served by the peculiar constitutional ca-
cophony that characterizes the conduct of our foreign affairs.

6
The Reins of Liberty—
Congress, the President,
and American Security

Edmund S. Muskie

The debate over who makes American foreign policy has been going on for more than two hundred years. Questions about the relative and rightful roles of Congress and the president have been raised each time the two institutions have come into conflict over a foreign policy decision.

The shifting positions taken by individuals and institutions underscores the fact that there are no firm, eternal truths in this area. At times, for example, the "conservative" position has been to uphold the constitutional predominance of Congress over the overreaching executive. Witness the Bricker Amendment of 1954—conservative Senator John Bricker's proposal to restrict the president's power to negotiate international agreements. At other times, though, including our own, "conservatives" have tended to make sweeping assertions of the overwhelming, rightful—and sole—powers of the president in foreign affairs.

Conflict in this area should come as no surprise. The founders had their own conflicts over the division of power in foreign policy. They were unwilling, and probably unable, explicitly to divide foreign policy powers between the legislative and the executive branches, or to cede supremacy in this arena either to Congress or to the president. Instead, they created a system of overlapping and competing powers—a system, in the words of Edwin Corwin, that was "an invitation to struggle" between the branches. Although a precise division of roles and powers cannot be divined in the founders' intentions, however, it is clear that they envisioned a vigorous and significant role for the Congress in foreign policy—not only the power of the purse but also the power to declare war and the Senate's unique responsibilities over treaties and appointments.

The Role of Congress

It has become difficult to discuss the role of Congress in setting national security policy because two caricatures of the president and Congress dominate our discussion of the subject. In one caricature we see the Congress as a quarrelsome throng of 535 backseat drivers— local politicians who imagine themselves the secretary of state. In the other caricature, we see a seriously misguided president (who might be named Johnson, Nixon, Carter, or Reagan, depending upon who is drawing the caricature), lured by a deep personality flaw, bad advice, or lack of understanding into a dangerous situation from which only Congress can extricate us.

We love to overdraw these caricatures; political cartoonists and talk show hosts have put their children through college on them. Unfortunately, these popular images would not be so widely held if they did not have some basis in the truth of our recent history.

Because most of my years in public service were spent in Congress, I am generally sympathetic with the prerogatives of the legislative branch on substantive decisions about arms control, covert action, and war powers. I have seen troubling abuses of the congressional role in formulating national security policy, however, as in 1987, when the Senate added eighty-six amendments to the Department of State authorization bill, among them requirements that the State Department merge embassies in the Caribbean and close down the Palestinian Liberation Organization's office at the United Nations.

The decline of political parties and the growing individualization of Congress can make such abuses more frequent and more worrisome. Once only a few House and Senate leaders and committee chairmen had sufficient national influence to participate in the planning of foreign policy. Today all it takes is an immodest amount of financial and intellectual resources, along with ready access to the media, for a junior member of Congress to develop a political identity independent of his party. While today's congressional leaders are not, as many suppose, lesser men than the giants whom presidents turned to for bipartisan support in previous national crises, they are lesser figures on Capitol Hill because their power has been diluted.

Presidential leadership has also been diluted greatly over the past quarter-century. Before President Ronald Reagan was elected in 1980, it was fashionable to speak of a succession of presidencies destroyed or crippled by the cumulative effects of the war in Vietnam, the Watergate affair, and the hostage-taking in Iran. Americans of both parties looked to Reagan to change this pattern, and for a time, especially after his overwhelming reelection in 1984, it appeared that he would. "Ronald Reagan has found the American sweet spot," *Time* magazine said of him in 1985. "The 75-year-old man is hitting home runs. . . . He grins his boyish grin and bobs his head in the way he has and trots around the bases." Where *Time* saw Reagan as an athletic superstar, *Fortune* elevated Reagan's hands-off managerial style to one that all businesspeople should emulate.

Just sixteen months later, however, after the initial revelations about the sale of arms to Iran, *Time*'s cover story asked, "Who's in charge? The nation calls for leadership and there is no one home."

Both the executive and the legislative branches are today far weaker than even twenty years ago. In their weakened conditions, the leaders at both ends of Pennsylvania Avenue need to help each other more than ever; instead, their relationship is more adversarial than ever. On crucial issues of national security, it is not surprising that Congress will sometimes question the president's judgment and the quality of the advice he receives. If the president's decisions seem flawed, Congress will inevitably assert its prerogatives. Presidents have a different perspective. They see Congress encroaching on their authority, and they fear that whenever Congress is granted a share of executive power, it will never relinquish it voluntarily.

Although the framers of the Constitution did not envision this merciless battle between weakened, caricatured institutions, the basis for their struggle is found in that document. The Constitution makes clear that each branch of government has a role to play but is not explicit about how those roles are applied in the real world. Leaders of the two branches must work out the practical aspects of their relationship for themselves, striving to balance constitutional prerogatives with the need for effective governance.

Checks and Balances

The government created in 1787 found order in the ingenious checks and balances among the several branches—none of which was more central than the restraints on executive power. Even Alexander Hamilton was at pains to emphasize the modest nature of the presidency. In *Federalist* No. 67, he wrote that the chief executive's powers were "in few instances greater, in some instances less, than those of a governor of New York."

In *Federalist* No. 75, Hamilton made the same point with specific reference to foreign policy:

The history of human conduct does not warrant that exalted opinion of human virtue which would make it wise in a nation to commit interests of so delicate and momentous a kind, as those which concern its intercourse with the rest of the world, to the sole disposal of a magistrate created and circumstanced as would be a president of the United States.

Foreign policy in a democracy runs many risks—the risk of paralyzing dissension among its citizens, the risk of duplicity by less scrupulous regimes, and the risk of premature disclosure of delicate negotiations. Those risks, however, pale in significance compared with the danger that arises when democracy's servants arrogate to themselves the power to ignore constitutional restraints. Those restraints give life and meaning to the idea of self-government.

Particularly in the actions of a few presidential aides involved in Iran-contra arms scandal, Americans saw that threat to democracy become real. Zeal replaced judgment, single-minded commitment to one policy goal encouraged end runs around the law, and physical courage became an excuse for political arrogance. Neither sound policy nor political consensus could have survived in these circumstances.

The sharp conflicts between the branches revealed in the Iran-contra scandal made clearer than ever the need to get our bearings straight and adjust the course of foreign policy planning. The two sides in this debate have frequently and articulately staked out their positions. Some justify executive unilateralism as a necessary evil to protect the United States in a world of unprecedented danger. Others fear the concentration of power in the presidency and look to Congress to contain the excesses that arose in the national security bureaucracy in 1985 and 1986.

Although these positions may at first seem irreconcilable, our constitutional record is encouraging. In numerous instances, the two branches have forged strong bonds and shaped farsighted policy.

The first treaty negotiated under the new Constitution provides a good example. The Jay Treaty of 1795 was far from satisfactory, even to President George Washington. His emissary John Jay had exceeded his instructions on some points and had fallen short of Washington's goals in the negotiations with the British. The president knew that the pact would arouse high emotions and much controversy. Nevertheless, he sent the agreement to the Senate, along with Jay's secret dispatches and instructions. The Senate in turn deliberated in executive session and offered its advice and consent to all but one article, on which the British eventually relented. The episode of the Jay Treaty offers a model of mutual respect between the president and the Senate.

The most passionate advocates of executive supremacy point out that Washington refused to share the confidential diplomatic papers with the House of Representatives. The House, however, requested these materials months after the Senate had already received the same materials and acted on them. Washington rejected the House request on the grounds that the Constitution confined the making of treaties to the president and the Senate. In responding to the House, Washington said that he might have acted differently if the House had stated a specific constitutional purpose for the materials—if, for example, the House had been seeking information for an impeachment proceeding.

Contrary to those who cite this episode as an instance of executive dominance, the Jay Treaty precedent shows how to make the constitutional system work by building confidence between the Capitol and the White House. It offers no support for the idea that presidents are free to withhold information from Congress. In fact, Washington specifically dropped from his message to the House a proposed assertion of more sweeping executive power. He had met his constitutional obligation by dealing straightforwardly and openly with the Senate. He chose not to undermine that success by seeking to inflate the president's power.

The Twentieth Century

Similarly, in this century gifted leaders in both branches have made the bond between Congress and the president effective and productive, even if it has not always been amiable. Particularly in the months before World War II, Franklin Roosevelt's vigor and vision enabled him to rally the Congress to policies that were controversial, but essential. Roosevelt was, in the memorable phrase of James McGregor Burns, both "lion" and "fox"; but in mobilizing the country and dealing with Congress, he used neither blunt power nor deviousness, but careful, cooperative persuasion.

When Roosevelt planned to trade aging destroyers to Great Britain in exchange for base rights, he acted openly on the basis of statutory authority. He even published Attorney General Robert Jackson's opinion in support of the swap just weeks before the 1940 election in which voters were to appraise his stewardship in keeping us out of the European war. Months before the Japanese attack on Pearl Harbor, Roosevelt earned approval for conscription and for the Lend-Lease program—both deeply controversial—by making his case forthrightly to Congress and to the country.

The more notable foreign policy successes of later presidents were also generally the result of active cooperation between the branches. That was the way Harry Truman gained support for the United Nations charter, the Marshall Plan, and the North Atlantic Treaty. Dwight Eisenhower enjoyed a steady and invaluable partnership with congressional leaders of the other party, including House Speaker Sam Rayburn and Senate Majority Leader Lyndon Johnson. John F. Kennedy, elected by the slimmest of margins, nonetheless persuaded an overwhelming Senate majority to support his Limited Nuclear Test Ban Treaty of 1963, the most enduring diplomatic achievement of his brief presidency.

Even Richard Nixon's historic opening to China was not so much the triumph of secret diplomacy as many would have us believe. It would not have been possible without a series of path-breaking hearings conducted by Senator William Fulbright in the mid-1960s. After years of congressional opposition to any dealings with the People's Republic of China, those hearings in the Foreign Relations Committee brought about a fundamental change in attitudes. They made President Nixon's initiatives toward Beijing not only wise statecraft, but good politics as well.

Restrictions on Foreign Policy

As we seek to lessen the frictions over foreign policy, we must not only recall these instances in which the system has worked and worked well but also reflect on the paradox that our founders understood and built into the constitutional scheme: on occasion, the system works best by failing to work, that is, by failing to reach a settled conclusion to policy disputes between the branches.

During the Nixon years, there were protracted debates concerning the possible deployment of antiballistic missile defenses. Congress never declined to fund the work on such defenses, but it slowed the program and debated its merits at great length. Eventually, this sparked negotiations to limit both U.S. and Soviet missile defenses. We now know that congressional reticence and the Anti-Ballistic Missile Treaty of 1972 spared the nation a multibillion dollar white elephant that even proponents admit would not have worked.

The possibility of a defense against nuclear missiles remains a hotly contested subject between the president and Congress. In seeking to reinterpret the 1972 pact to allow testing as part of the Strategic Defense Initiative, President Reagan reached an impasse between the two branches, an impasse that would not have arisen if the president had consulted with congressional leaders during his administration's deliberations over the interpretation.

The administration's reinterpretation stood logic on its head, as senators who had participated in the ratification could have told administration officials, had those legislators been asked. The administration also declined to consult with all but one of the original negotiators of the treaty and did not involve the Soviets in private discussions to resolve ambiguities in the treaty. The Reagan administration simply declared that the explanation of the treaty given to the Senate by one administration was not what the treaty really meant. How could the Senate take seriously its constitutional obligation to consider and ratify treaties based on the executive branch's explanation, given such a radical reinterpretation? It is no wonder that the Senate refused to allow its constitutional role to be subverted in this way.

Just as the original conflict over antiballistic missile defenses during the Nixon administration preceded the 1972 treaty, however, the conflict over reinterpretation of that pact coincided with a remarkable period of progress on arms control, a period during which both the United States and the Soviet Union continued to comply with the traditional interpretation of the ABM treaty and with most of the provisions of the SALT II agreement. More important, the Soviets began to consider deep cuts in their nuclear arsenal that led to the INF treaty and the START talks on reduction of strategic arms. Without the staunch support for the original ABM treaty on Capitol Hill, the Soviets would not have been likely to agree to these cuts, because the long-term process of nuclear arms reduction is impossible without previous agreement on defensive deployments.

The extended conflict between the branches over the interpretation of the ABM pact might have hurt our standing around the world with countries that had expected us to live by our word and not to play word games with mutually binding obligations. It did not hurt our negotiating position with the Soviets, though, and might well have helped us begin to make progress on arms control. By refusing to concede the administration's radical alteration of the ABM pact, the Senate provided the essential element of stability to our foreign policy. Even when the two branches cannot resolve their differences, those continuing conflicts can make our policies more stable, reliable, and predictable than they would be if one branch called all the shots.

War Powers. The War Powers Resolution, enacted over President Nixon's veto, is another subject of continued, unresolved conflict between the two branches. That conflict, too, has helped keep our policies stable and reliable, ensuring that the profound decision to use military force will not be taken lightly and balancing vigorous executive capacity with prudent legislative restraint.

Many consider the War Powers Resolution an example of Congress's asserting its prerogatives without due regard for the authority of the president, depriving the president of the flexibility needed to respond quickly in a time of crisis. The law, though, allows the president to use our armed forces in emergencies, as long as Congress is notified and congressional approval obtained before the military engagement becomes as deep and sustained as our involvement in Vietnam. Contrast this approach with the Ludlow Amendment, a 1938 proposal that would have required a national referendum before war could be declared, except in the most extreme cases. This amendment was defeated in the House of Representatives after vigorous lobbying by Franklin Roosevelt.

The War Powers Resolution was intended to restore the distinction between the power to declare war and the power to make war that was deliberately made at the Constitutional Convention. At one point during the drafting, the Constitution gave the Congress the power to "make" war. James Madison and Elbridge Gerry noted that the executive should have the power to repel sudden attacks and moved to change the word for Congress's power to "declare."

Although in theory this distinction between Congress's power to declare war and the president's to conduct that war as commander in chief remains in force, a very different arrangement developed after World War II. The last time an American president asked Congress to declare war was after the Japanese attack on Pearl Harbor. Our prolonged involvement in Vietnam served as the impetus for this legislation, but it was not merely a reflexive response to the long, undeclared war. Members of Congress agonized over how presidential and congressional prerogatives could best be shared in light of the conditions of modern warfare. The authors of the bill (of whom I was one) did not wish to amend or alter the Constitution; they were searching for new ways to fulfill the clear intent of its framers.

The War Powers Resolution recognizes that the most critical decision is the decision to commit troops to a situation in the first place. When that initial decision is not well conceived, when the problem is not one that U.S. combat units can solve, it can be very difficult for either the president in Washington or military leaders in the field to extricate our troops without embarrassment or excessive casualties. We learned this lesson when we watched the helicopters lifting our personnel from the U.S. embassy before the fall of Saigon. The Soviets perhaps learned a similar lesson during their futile decade of fighting in Afghanistan.

The best way to avoid such national tragedies is to avoid that first lapse of judgment. By requiring that the decision be accounted for to

Congress, the War Powers Resolution ensures that the reasoning behind the first decision to commit troops is sound and can be logically explained. Even if Congress vehemently disagrees, the president can keep our troops in place for another sixty days and thirty days after that if needed.

The War Powers Resolution itself is not responsible for the debate over the use of troops that arose in 1987 after the Reagan administration posted U.S. ships in the Persian Gulf. Instead, the legislation makes us face up to the clear meaning of our Constitution and the requirement for communication and comity between the executive and the legislative branches. Communication and comity lead to sound and stable policy.

Secrecy. One of the most perplexing challenges to constitutional governance of foreign policy stems from the need for secrecy. National security affairs often require discretion; negotiations must be confidential while under way, and some operations must be covert. We can never allow secrecy to make those negotiations or operations immune from accountability, however. That requires a reasonable blend of executive confidentiality and discreet legislative oversight. The frequent assertion that Congress is an unreliable overseer of secret matters and incapable of keeping sensitive information to itself is belied by the responsible performance of nearly all legislators.

Those serving on the House and Senate Intelligence Committees, for example, have proven themselves to be dependable partners of the intelligence agencies they must hold accountable. The committees have evaluated the most highly classified intelligence collected by the United States and reviewed dozens of covert operations, without leaking substantive intelligence data. Deliberate leaks as well as accidental disclosures will be a problem as long as our diplomacy is conducted by human beings, but the executive branch fully shares in the responsibility for such occurrences. For the president's aides, "leakmanship" is one more weapon in the contest to tilt the president toward a particular policy, to frustrate a policy one opposes, to advance one's career, or to frustrate the career advancement of another. Judging from his aborted proposal to submit even members of his cabinet to lie-detector tests, President Reagan evidently recognized this fact.

A regard for the Constitution always requires us to guard against the tendency to exploit secrecy for domestic politics. All too often, we have seen the practice of secrecy shift away from legitimate purposes of foreign policy to shield officials from political criticism. Ironically, this concern for secrecy has sometimes affected most those administrations that would seem to need it least—presidencies grounded in exceptional popular support.

(There may be something to the thesis that extraordinary electoral mandates tempt presidents into error. The tendency to overreach showed up in Franklin Roosevelt's second term, after the landslide of 1936. Lyndon Johnson's overwhelming victory in 1964 may have contributed to his presumption of greater legislative deference than his foreign policy eventually earned. Richard Nixon's 1972 triumph may have exacerbated the attitudes that contaminated his abbreviated second term. And Ronald Reagan's team may have grown overconfident and insensitive to congressional perspectives when he won so overwhelmingly in 1984; certainly the Iran-contra scandal took shape within a few months after the election.)

Conclusion

Those who believe that more active congressional involvement in foreign policy will only enfeeble the presidency underestimate the strength that can flow from adherence to the constitutional design. Shared responsibility between the branches should spare us some of the more foolish schemes that have slipped through the executive decision-making process—from ludicrous chemical assaults on Fidel Castro's beard in the 1960s to the mining of Nicaraguan harbors in the 1980s. The United States has not been served by such unsupervised executive branch schemes, but embarrassed.

In the area of covert operations, most of the successful ones of recent years have been those that enjoyed prior congressional approval. When officials have withheld notification from Congress, as in the case of the mining of the Nicaraguan harbors, the operations have often been failures. It is not that notifying Congress somehow makes an operation successful but that the operations that officials do not want to explain to Congress are those that cannot articulately be explained or defended, usually because they are ill-conceived initially. Congress is an important filter for such ideas, and given the number of them that have cropped up in our lifetimes, it is a very necessary filter.

The Constitution mandates a perpetual search for a sound working relationship between the two governing branches, one in which elected officials understand that they serve the people best by working together. As President Gerald R. Ford put it, Congress and the president should form a "good marriage," not just a honeymoon followed by years of antagonism. Neither branch can build such a marriage by attempting to subjugate or ignore the other. This simple truth applies to policies and operations not only in the darker reaches of national security but also in the public realm of conflicts over budget and program priorities for defense, trade-offs among foreign aid programs, and various approaches to trade policy.

Former Secretary of State George P. Shultz struck the right theme when he identified trust as the coin of the realm. No Congress can cooperate with an executive whose words it does not trust. No president can confide in a Congress that violates his confidence. The sad experience of the mid-1980s should not cause us to lose faith in the possibility of accommodation between the legislative and the executive branches. It is an object lesson in the obligation of each branch to warrant the other's trust.

More than a century ago, Lord Macaulay wrote condescendingly that the American Constitution was "all sail and no anchor." This vivid image was wrong then, and we can only hope that it remains wrong. The Constitution deserves a more suitable metaphor, one that reflects its unique ability to harness the institutions of government to the service of the American people. Perhaps it is more like a plow, with Congress and the president bound together to pull the load. The ties that bind them together are not the chains of subjugation. They are the reins of liberty.

7

Congressional Overreaching in Foreign Policy

Dick Cheney

The eight years of President Ronald Reagan's administration were a rocky period for legislative-executive relations in foreign policy. Broadly speaking, the sharper the disagreement between congressional Democrats and the Republican president over substantive issues, the more likely were those disagreements to spill over into procedural and constitutional turf battles. The procedural fights would raise institutional jealousies that would feed back to harm substantive policies.

In the early months of President George Bush's administration, as these words were being written, it appeared that players on both ends of Pennsylvania Avenue were trying to tone down the institutional rhetoric. The president, the Speaker of the House, and the majority leader of the Senate were all talking about the need for bipartisanship. Far be it for me to dissent here from this salutary tone. Nevertheless, we do have to prepare for eventualities. Sooner or later, under this president or a future one, some foreign policy issue is bound to provoke a sharp disagreement between the White House and Congress. Before that day comes, it is important to reflect on the institutional issues raised by the clashes just past.

This essay is about patterns of congressional overreaching during the Reagan administration. By choosing that subject, I do not mean to suggest that overreaching was limited to Capitol Hill. Anyone who followed the Iran-contra affair knows that was not so. Congressional aggrandizement, however, does seem less generally understood, more systemic, and more institutionally ingrained than its White House counterpart. Members of Congress may be asking for bipar-

---

This paper was prepared for an American Enterprise Institute conference, "Foreign Policy and the Constitution," held March 14–15, 1989. It was written before Mr. Cheney was nominated to be secretary of defense. It should be read, therefore, as a statement of his personal views.—Ed.

tisanship, but they have not given up what I would consider some of the more problematic aspects of their institutional self-understanding.

Posing the Issue

Congress and the president both have important roles to play in shaping the conduct of U.S. foreign policy. Both must be involved for any major policy to be successful over the long term. But this does not mean that all forms of joint participation work equally well. The odds for success become much worse if either branch steps beyond its institutional competence. It is crucial, therefore, to understand (1) just what the institutional competence of each branch is; (2) what the connection is between institutional competence and constitutional authority; (3) how Congress, in an attempt to force joint participation, has overstepped the bounds of its competence and authority in recent years; and (4) why this has been harmful.

The point of these questions is to get beyond the usual legal arguments to look at the practical consequences of abusing the separation of powers. (I refer readers interested in the legal and constitutional history to the relevant chapters in the Iran-contra committees' minority report.)[1] The problem with most legal arguments is that they tend to become debates about the precise application of this or that group of words. In too many judicial opinions the Constitution appears almost as if it were a collection of disembodied clauses, each with its own legal history, parceling power every which way. But individual clauses are not the best prisms for viewing the separation of powers, a subject suffusing the whole Constitution.

The Constitution does not really distribute powers at random; it is not simply an "invitation to struggle."[2] It does give the separate branches distinct levers for influencing the same set of policy decisions, but the struggle for influence was not supposed to be a free-for-all. The powers are separated, and the levers of influence conferred, according to a consistent set of underlying principles.

Broadly speaking, the Congress was intended to be a collective, deliberative body. When working at its best, it would slow down decisions, improve their substantive content, subject them to compromise, and help build a consensus behind general rules before they were to be applied to the citizenry. The presidency, in contrast, was designed as a one-person office to ensure that it would be ready for action. Its major characteristics, in the language of *Federalist* No. 70, were to be "decision, activity, secrecy and dispatch."[3]

Each branch, in other words, was designed to have a specific set of characteristics that were meant to go together with specific kinds of jobs. Collective bodies are important for deliberation; one-person bodies are better for decision, energy, secrecy, and dispatch. Deliberation and action are both important. Both will be brought to bear in all major policy arenas. But the framers knew that the capacities to act and to deliberate are not equally important for all aspects of every job.

When Congress stays within its capacities, it can be a helpful participant in formulating policy. But in recent years, in a wide range of disagreements with the president, Congress has used policy levers that go well beyond those the Constitution intended for the legislative branch. The issue is not limited to a formal violation of a parchment document. When Congress steps beyond its capacities, it takes traits that can be helpful to collective deliberation and turns them into a harmful blend of vacillation, credit claiming, blame avoidance, and indecision. The real world effect often turns out, as Caspar Weinberger has said, to be not a transfer of power from the president to the Congress but a denial of power to the government as a whole.[4]

The following pages examine three policy areas: diplomacy, covert operations, and war powers. In all three, congressional over-reaching has systematic policy effects. It is important to be clear at the outset that my argument is about systematic effects, not individual policy disagreements. For example, Congress's efforts to dictate diplomatic bargaining tactics, as well as efforts by individual members to conduct back-channel negotiations of their own, make it extremely difficult for the country to sustain a consistent bargaining posture for an extended time, whoever the president and whatever the policy. In intelligence the problem goes beyond consistency to a more basic conflict between action and inaction. One proposal made in the wake of Iran-contra would have required the president to notify Congress of all covert actions within forty-eight hours, without any exceptions. By refusing to allow the president any leeway, no matter how urgent the circumstances, that proposal would have set up a direct conflict between Congress's procedural requirements and the president's constitutional obligation to act.

The War Powers Act combines both these problems in one statute. Just as congressional diplomacy tilts the balance away from patient diplomacy, so does the War Powers Act tilt the balance away from a patient, measured application of force toward either a quick strike or inaction. And just as requiring forty-eight-hour notification for all covert operations favors inaction over action in rare but important circumstances, so does the War Powers Act favor inaction over measured action in the more common circumstances in which that act might be applied. In all these cases the underlying issues are the same: the relationships between deliberation and action and between procedure and substance. To explain why, let us begin with congressional diplomacy.

Congressional Diplomacy

Congressional diplomacy has two aspects: (1) Congress's attempts to tie the president's negotiating hands and (2) back-channel negotiations conducted by some leading members of Congress with foreign governments. The first is familiar and will therefore be treated more briefly. I shall concentrate on one major issue to illustrate, but any of a dozen would do just as well.

Instructing the President. In 1987 and 1988 the House of Representatives added provisions to the defense authorization bill that would have required the president to abide by provisions of the unratified, decade-old Strategic Arms Limitation Treaty between the United States and the Soviet Union (SALT II). Although the House bills did not mention SALT II by name, they tried to prohibit the president from deploying weapons that would have taken our nuclear arsenals above three of the treaty's "sublimits" for submarines, missiles, and bombers. The Senate rejected the House's sublimits in both years, but House and Senate conferees required the president to retire old submarines to keep the U.S. warhead total near the overall SALT II limit.

President Reagan opposed the restriction in both years because (1) the Soviet Union was violating other aspects of the SALT II treaty, (2) the Soviet Union was deploying 30 percent more multiple warhead missiles (820) than the United States (550), (3) the president was in the midst of trying to negotiate a 50 percent reduction of nuclear arms in a Strategic Arms Reduction Treaty (START), and (4) unilateral adherence to SALT II would have undercut the president's negotiating position in the START talks. For tactical reasons the president was willing to sign a bill in 1987 that required him to retire one old submarine. But in 1988 he decided to veto the authorization bill to make a principled defense of his position during an election year. House Democrats backed down, but they did not change their views about the propriety of the original bill.

No one can dispute Congress's constitutional power to decide what weapons should be funded. The issue therefore is one not of constitutional law but of Congress's willingness to second-guess the president's bargaining tactics. To put the point bluntly, liberal Democrats doubted the president was telling the truth when he said he was trying to negotiate a verifiable arms treaty that would include major reductions. They seemed to believe that the best way to negotiate a treaty was to place limits on our side and then politely ask the Soviet Union to follow.

At least they were consistent. The framework almost exactly paralleled that in 1982, when liberal Democrats in the House failed by two votes to pass a nuclear freeze resolution that would have prevented us from deploying intermediate-range missiles in Europe, even though the Soviets had already deployed similar missiles of their own. At that time House Democrats said that deployment would make the Russians angry and break up intermediate nuclear force (INF) negotiations. The president believed that deployment had to come before negotiations would bear fruit. That is, the Soviets had to understand that our defenses would be strong even if there were no agreement; this would give them a reason to talk. President Reagan's view prevailed—very, very narrowly. The missiles were deployed, the Soviet Union returned to the bargaining table, and in 1988 a treaty was ratified that for the first time banned a whole class of nuclear weapons from the arsenals of both major superpowers.

There is an important lesson here that goes beyond the specific issue. Congress is simply not well equipped to take budget tools that are perfectly appropriate for some kinds of issues and use them as levers for dictating bargaining tactics to the president. President Reagan's record on INF shows that negotiating success requires a willingness to stick patiently to a tough strategy. But patience, or the willingness to stand pat, is in reality a form of decisive action. It is the kind of action a single person is better able to take over time than a collective body. Congress finds it tough to speak with one voice. It is made up of 535 people. Most of them have to stand for reelection every two years. Because of this, a significant number at any given moment, on any given issue, are looking for quick results—for something to show the voters before the next election.

It would be smarter, therefore, for Congress not to use its formal lawmaking capacity to pressure presidential negotiations. Yes, presidents have to consult with members of Congress. Whether presidents like it or not, the Senate does get to vote on ratification, and both chambers may be needed for implementing legislation. Any negotiation that does not pay attention to these constraints is a negotiation that is headed for trouble. But consultation, advice, and influence are far removed from binding instructions conveyed through formal legislative acts. Meaningful consultation means giving advice while keeping the power to withhold consent in reserve. It is foolish for Congress to think it can force a negotiation to move forward, and there is time enough for formal action after a negotiation is finished.

Members as Diplomats. As troubling as congressional negotiating instructions may be, they pale when compared with the disturbing tendency of some members to conduct their own back-channel negotiations with foreign leaders. Increasingly, members of Congress have set themselves up as alternative secretaries of state. Senators and representatives from both parties have crossed the line separating what I would consider legitimate legislative fact finding from the realm of diplomatic communication. Some recent examples will show how serious the problem has become.

The Speaker and Nicaragua. The Speaker of the House symbolically represents the House's understanding of its role. The first example, therefore, is about his actions at one of the many potential turning points in negotiations between the Communist government of Nicaragua and the Nicaraguan democratic resistance.

The Organization of American States (OAS) was scheduled to meet in Washington in the middle of November 1987. On November 9, a few days before the OAS sessions, President Reagan announced for the first time that the United States would be willing to negotiate security issues with Nicaragua, but only if the representatives of four other Central American countries were also involved. The question of direct United States–Nicaragua talks had been a sticky one for some time. The Sandinistas were trying to portray the resistance as puppets of the United States. Their aim was to negotiate a deal that would cut off U.S. support for the contras in return for a promise that the Nicaraguan government would not export arms to the Communists in El Salvador and elsewhere. Left out of the Sandinista equation would have been any limitations on the military support Nicaragua had been receiving from the Soviet Union and Cuba and any meaningful reforms that would move the Managua regime toward genuine political freedom.

President Reagan's statement on November 9 was a carefully measured response to the continuing stalemate. The president was saying that we are, and always have been, open to discussing some issues directly with Nicaragua and the other countries of Central America but that Nicaragua's main dispute is not with us. The Sandinistas still ought to begin direct talks with the contras to negotiate a domestic political settlement conducive to pluralism and political freedom.

At this point the Speaker of the House, James Wright, entered the picture. Here is *Congressional Quarterly's* description of the next few days.

> At his ornate office in the Capitol, Wright met with [Nicaraguan President Daniel] Ortega for more than an hour on

Nov. 11. The next day, he met with Ortega again for nearly an hour, then spent about 90 minutes with three members of the Contra "directorate," the civilian leadership of the guerrilla force. Wright talked later in the day with Cardinal [Miguel] Obando [y Bravo] after he arrived in Washington from Managua.

On Nov. 13, Wright travelled to the Vatican Embassy in Washington for a final 90-minute session between Ortega and Cardinal Obando. At that session, Ortega gave the Cardinal a copy of his government's multi-point plan for a cease-fire. . . .

[Representative David E.] Bonior [Democrat-Michigan], the House chief deputy majority whip, was the only other member of Congress at Wright's sessions with the Nicaraguans.

In his sessions with Ortega, Wright apparently discussed in detail the Nicaraguan's proposal for implementing a cease-fire. Sources said the plan originally contained nearly 20 points but was eventually reduced to 11 points, partly as a result of the Wright-Ortega discussions.[5]

These three days of meetings were clearly a series of negotiations, under any ordinary understanding of that term. Interestingly, they were conducted in secret, without including or adequately informing the State Department. After the sessions were over, the Sandinista leader crowed to the press on November 13 that his dealings with Wright would "leave the Administration totally isolated."[6]

Other members and Nicaragua. Speaker Wright's meetings of November 1987 were not isolated examples. Unfortunately, they built upon, and helped lend a sense of legitimacy to, a growing pattern of legislative branch intrusions into a field that was clearly intended to be executive. Consider two other examples involving Nicaragua.

In April 1985 the House decided against contra aid by two votes. The next week Ortega took a trip to Moscow. His trip was a public relations fiasco for House Democrats who had voted against the contras. Shortly afterward Representatives Bonior and George Miller (Democrat-California) visited Managua, where they were reported to have held a series of meetings with government officials and to have barred U.S. embassy officials from attending. According to one unnamed House Democratic leader who was quoted in a press account, the meetings were "dangerously close to negotiations." The point, according to the press report, was to inform the Sandinistas that unless their government took steps toward pluralism, some congressional Democrats would be likely to switch votes and support contra aid.[7]

Members of Congress do not need a personal meeting to intrude

107

in the realm of diplomacy. On March 20, 1984, while the United States was still legally aiding the contras, ten House Democrats—including Wright, then majority leader, Michael Barnes, chairman of the Western Hemisphere subcommittee of the Foreign Affairs Committee, and other prominent members—sent the famous (or infamous) "Dear Commandante" letter to Ortega. After declaring their opposition to contra aid, the signers said, "We want to commend you and the members of your government for taking steps to open up the political process of your country." Although those steps were barely visible and clearly opportunistic, the signers went on to urge Ortega to continue what he had started to "strengthen the hands of those in our country who desire better relations."[8] In other words, the letter was telling Ortega how to behave to strengthen the legislative position of those members of Congress who were opposed to what was then the position of the legislative as well as the executive branch.

More members, other countries. Then in 1985 there was the remarkable letter to Prime Minister Wilfried Martens of Belgium. The letter, from thirteen nonleadership Democrats, was delivered to Martens during the prime minister's state visit to the United States.[9] It mistakenly praised a (nonexistent) "recent announcement by your Government to delay the initial deployment of Cruise missiles in your country." In fact, as one newspaper column noted, Martens strongly supported deployment against strong domestic political opposition.[10] As it turned out, the missiles were deployed, and their deployment was an essential building block in negotiating the INF Treaty with the Soviet Union. But the point is not that these members of Congress had their facts wrong. The point is that they stepped beyond the normal, legitimate realm of domestic debate to communicate directly with another government in an attempt to influence that government to oppose U.S. policy.

The problem, as I said earlier, is not limited to one party. One former Republican House member who stepped over what I think are appropriate lines was George Hansen of Idaho. Hansen made a ten-day visit to Tehran in November 1979, two weeks after more than sixty Americans were taken hostage in the U.S. embassy. His aim, Hansen said at the time, was to "get in on an unofficial basis and do business."[11]

Nor is the problem confined to the House. During the Iran-contra hearings the House and Senate investigating committees received a series of 1986 State Department cables about American citizens who were alleged to be visiting Eden Pastora "at [the] request of Sen. Jesse Helms." Pastora at that time was a contra leader based south of

Nicaragua. According to one of the cables (from Central America to Washington), the Americans agreed that the United States would send supplies to Pastora in return for his willingness to undertake specific activities on behalf of the Nicaraguan resistance. In reply, the State Department fired back that it was "astounded" because the private citizens were "not in a position to commit the U.S. government."[12]

A recurring problem. The problem of private diplomacy is not new. In 1798 Dr. George Logan was accused of meddling in negotiations between the United States and France. Although the facts were disputed, he was suspected by many Federalists of having been a secret envoy sent to France to represent the Jeffersonian Democrats. In response Congress passed a law the next year that made it criminal for any citizen of the United States, without the permission of the U.S. government,

> directly or indirectly [to] commence, or carry on, any verbal or written correspondence or intercourse with any foreign government, or any agent or officer thereof, with an intent to influence the measures or conduct of any foreign government, or of any officer or agent thereof, in relation to any disputes or controversies with the United States, or defeat the measures of the government of the United States.

The only exception in the act was for individuals seeking to redress a personal injury to themselves.[13]

The Logan Act is still a part of the U.S. Code, with only minor grammatical changes.[14] Although the act was aimed at the most obvious level against private citizens, congressional debate at the time made it clear that the function belonged to the executive branch, and outrage was expressed not only at Logan's role but at the alleged support he received from members of the opposition political party who did not have the president's blessing. It is significant, as the noted constitutional historian Charles Warren wrote when he was assistant attorney general, that the more than two hundred pages of debate about the act are printed in the *Annals of Congress* under the heading "Usurpation of Executive Authority."[15]

Unfortunately, political and legal difficulties have made the Logan Act all but a dead letter. As a result it is important to find a less confrontational, more enforceable way to restore the president's constitutional role as the sole organ of diplomacy. To meet that objective, some of us drafted a measure in 1988 that would have required members of Congress to report any communications with foreign representatives within forty-eight hours after they occur. This modest proposal might not prevent individual members from overstepping the bounds, but at least it would ensure that the government's only official channel knows what is going on.

The basic issue is not about a reporting requirement, however. Congress's diplomatic interventions undermine the country's ability to act effectively in the international arena. Domestic disputes over foreign policy are fully legitimate, but the Constitution's framers were explicit about the dangers of projecting our internal disputes externally. Their debates referred to situations that almost exactly parallel the one in the "Dear Commandante" memorandum of 1984. Every foreign leader in a dispute with this country has an incentive to play upon divisions inside the United States. To the extent that we let members of Congress behave as if they were diplomats, we guarantee foreign opportunism under all future presidents of either party.

The United States needs to speak to other countries with one voice. Congress, by its nature, cannot do so. That is why the framers separated the foreign policy powers as they did. While some other constitutional issues may be in dispute, there can be no doubt that the president was meant to be the "sole organ"—the eyes, ears, and mouth—of this country's diplomacy.[16]

Covert Operations

The idea of a forty-eight-hour "reverse notification" for members of Congress was originally proposed as an amendment to an ill-advised attempt in 1988 to revise the Intelligence Oversight Act of 1980. Under the 1980 law all agencies and entities of the United States involved in intelligence activities are required to notify the House and Senate intelligence committees (or, under special conditions, the chairmen and ranking minority members of the two committees and four leaders of the House and Senate) before beginning any significant, anticipated intelligence activity. The law also contemplated, however, that under some conditions prior notice would not be given. In those situations, it required the president "to fully inform the intelligence committees in a timely fashion."

Under this law the intelligence committees have become significant players whose support any prudent administration would do well to encourage. The 1980 law did not challenge the president's inherent constitutional authority to initiate covert actions. In fact, that law specifically denied any intention to require advance congressional approval for such actions. Nevertheless, Congress does have a very strong lever for controlling any operation that lasts more than a short time.

Operations undertaken without prior approval must be limited to the funds available through a contingency fund. Constitutionally, Congress could abolish that fund and require project-by-project financing. Of course, such a decision would be suicidal because it would deprive the country of the ability to react quickly to breaking events. But because Congress does have this draconian power in principle, the intelligence committees can and do use the annual budget process to review every continuing operation. Any time Congress feels that an operation is unwise, it may step in to prohibit funds in the coming budget cycle from being used for that purpose. As a result all operations of extended duration have the committees' tacit support. Considering how many people in Congress and the general public have reservations about all covert operations, this is an important political base for any administration concerned about the country's long-term intelligence capabilities.

Proposed Forty-Eight-Hour Rule. The intelligence committees can review covert operations only if they know about them. President Reagan did not notify the intelligence committees of his administration's sales of arms to Iran in 1986 for almost eleven months after signing a formal finding to authorize them. I do not think anyone in Congress believes this was timely. The important question for the future is, How should Congress respond?

In 1988 the Senate passed and two House committees reported legislation that would have required the president under all conditions, with no exceptions, to notify Congress of covert operations within forty-eight hours of their start. Early in 1989 Speaker Wright announced that the bill would temporarily be shelved "as an opening gesture of good faith on our part" toward the new administration. But the Speaker specifically reserved the option to reintroduce the bill if the situation called for it.[17] Therefore, the underlying theoretical issues remain to be addressed.

At the heart of the dispute over requiring notification within forty-eight hours was a deeper one over the scope of the president's inherent constitutional power. I believe the president has the authority, without statute, to use the resources placed at his disposal to protect American lives abroad and to serve certain other important foreign policy objectives. The range of the president's discretion does vary, as Justice Robert H. Jackson said in his famous concurring opinion in the steel seizure case. When the president's actions are consonant with express congressional authorizations, discretion can be at its maximum. A middle range of power exists when Congress is silent. Presidential power is at its lowest ebb when it is directly

111

opposed to congressional mandate.[18] What is interesting about this typology, however, is that even when Congress speaks and the president's power is at its lowest, Jackson acknowledged that there are limits beyond which Congress cannot legislate.[19] Those limits are defined by the scope of the inviolable powers inherent in the presidential office.

Let me now apply this mode of analysis to the sphere of covert action. Congress was legislatively silent about covert action for most of American history, knowing full well that many broad-ranging actions had been undertaken at presidential initiative, with congressionally provided contingency funds.[20] For most of American history, therefore, presidents were acting in the middle range of the authority Jackson described. Congress does have the power, however, to control the money and material resources available to the president for covert actions. The 1980 oversight act and its predecessors after 1974 were attempts by Congress to place conditions on the president's use of congressionally provided resources. Those conditions, for the most part, have to do with providing information to Congress. Because Congress arguably cannot properly fulfill its legislative function on future money bills without information, the reporting requirements can be understood as logical and appropriate extensions of a legitimate legislative power.

The constitutional question is, What are the limits to what Congress may demand as an adjunct of its appropriations power? Broadly speaking, Congress may not use the money power to achieve purposes that it would be unconstitutional for it to achieve directly. It may not place a condition on the salaries of judges, for example, to prohibit the judges from spending any time (that is, any part of their salaries) to reach a particular constitutional conclusion.[21] In the same way, Congress may not use its clearly constitutional powers over executive branch resources and procedures to invade an inherently presidential power. For example, Congress may not use an appropriations rider to deprive the president of his authority as the "sole organ of diplomacy" to speak personally, or through any agent of his choice, with another government about any subject at all.

How would this reasoning apply to the proposed forty-eight-hour rule? Congress properly justified the 1980 notification requirement by the need for information as a necessary adjunct to the legislative power to appropriate money. By using this justification, Congress stood squarely within a line of cases upholding Congress's contempt power. In the 1821 case of *Anderson* v. *Dunn* the Supreme Court upheld the use of contempt as an implied power needed to implement others given expressly by the Constitution. In a statement that applies to all the government's branches, the Court said: "There is not in the whole of that admirable instrument, a grant of powers which does not draw after it others, not expressed, but vital to their exercise; not substantive and independent, indeed, but auxiliary and subordinate."[22]

Using this reasoning, the Court argued that even though courts were vested with the contempt power by statute, they would have been able to exercise that power without a statute. For the same reason, the Court held, Congress must have inherent authority to exercise a similar power.[23] Later cases tried to circumscribe Congress's contempt power, but the power was always held to be an adjunct to Congress's legislative functions and therefore to rest on an implied constitutional foundation.[24]

The Court's argument might seem to support Congress's implied right to demand information. But what happens if one branch's right to demand information confronts another implied power, equally well grounded on an explicit constitutional foundation, claimed by another of the government's branches? That was the issue in the executive privilege case of *U.S. v. Nixon*.[25] In that case we learned that the decision in any case will depend on the competing claims of the two branches at odds with each other.

The proposed forty-eight-hour bill explicitly recognized the president's inherent power to initiate covert actions. The 1980 oversight act and the forty-eight-hour bill both took pains to say that by requiring notification, Congress was not asserting a right to approve presidential decisions in advance. But if the president has the inherent power to initiate covert actions, then the same rule about implied powers that gives Congress the right to demand information also gives the president the implied powers he may need to put his acknowledged power into effect.

In most cases there is no conflict between the president's power to initiate an action and requiring him to notify the intelligence committees (or a smaller group of leaders) of that operation in advance. In a few very rare circumstances, however, there can be a direct conflict. Consider a clear-cut example from the Carter administration.

According to Admiral Stansfield Turner, who was director of central intelligence at the time, on three occasions, all occurring while Americans were being held hostage in Iran, President Jimmy Carter withheld notification during an operation. In each case, Turner said, "I would have found it very difficult to look . . . a person in the eye and tell him or her that I was going to discuss this life threatening mission with even half a dozen people in the CIA who did not absolutely have to know."[26] Of the three cases mentioned by Turner, the one that raised the key issue most directly occurred when notification was withheld for about three months until six Americans could be smuggled out of the Canadian embassy in Tehran. In that operation the Canadian government—whose own embassy was being placed at extreme risk—apparently made withholding notification a condition of its participation.[27] Since Congress cannot tell another government what risks that government should be willing to take with the safety of its personnel, the decision to go forward had to be made on Canada's terms or not at all. Under these conditions the president could not have fulfilled his constitutional obligation to protect American lives if he had insisted on notifying Congress within forty-eight hours.

The Iranian hostage examples show that the situations under which notification may have to be withheld depend not on how much time has elapsed but on the character of the operations.[28] There can be no question that when other governments place specific security requirements on cooperating with the United States, the no-exceptions aspect of the proposed forty-eight-hour rule would be equivalent to denying the president his constitutionally inherent power to act.

Leaks. Supporters of the forty-eight-hour bill tried to respond to the concerns about foreign government cooperation by sidestepping the precise issue and describing the concern about congressional leaks as ill founded. I wish that were so. It is true that President Reagan gave timely reports to the intelligence committees about every operation during his administration except the Iran arms sales and that most of the information was kept secure. It is wrong to suggest, however, that Congress is leak proof. An entire chapter of the minority report of the Iran-contra investigating committees was devoted to congressional leaks.[29]

It is bad enough when any member of Congress or staff person discloses classified information. It is far more serious when a leak comes from the so-called Gang of Eight (House and Senate intelligence committee chairmen and ranking minority members, Speaker and minority leader of the House, majority and minority leaders of the Senate).[30] This is the select group the oversight act designates for notification of operations considered too sensitive to be shared with the full committees. But the most remarkable situation of all comes when a member of this group tries to justify leaks as a matter of policy.

That is exactly what happened during the closing weeks of the 100th Congress. The forty-eight-hour bill never came up for House floor debate because of the public outcry over a possible leak by the Speaker of the House. At his daily press briefing on September 20, 1988, Speaker Wright told reporters: "We have received clear testimony from CIA people that they have deliberately done things to provoke an overreaction on the part of the government in Nicaragua."[31] Minority Leader Robert Michel and I sent a letter the next day to the House Select Committee on Standards of Official Conduct (the "ethics committee") asking it to investigate whether the Speaker had violated Rule 48 of the House, governing the disclosure of classified information.[32]

It would be wrong of me at this stage, before the ethics committee concludes its investigation, to comment on or speculate about whether a leak did occur.[33] Whatever the conclusion on this matter, however, the Speaker's immediate public response to the issue was troubling. "The fact that a matter is classified secret doesn't mean it's sacrosanct and immune from criticism," Wright told a group of reporters: "It is not only my right but my responsibility to express publicly my opposition to policies I think are wrong."[34] The premise underlying this statement is not new. At least one senator and one former member of the House have been quoted as saying similar things.[35] But familiarity in this case does not breed acceptance. If Congress is to have any role in overseeing covert operations, it must take seriously its responsibility to protect the information it receives. What Wright asserted was that it might be acceptable for a single member of Congress to blow a covert action, with all the danger that implies, by discussing it overtly.

Now consider the Speaker's stated position in light of (1) the characteristic differences between a legislature and an executive and (2) the fact that a decision to leak in effect is a decision to kill an operation. Virtually no policy of any consequence will have unanimous support in a democratic legislature. That may be good for deliberation but makes it very tough to maintain operational security. If more members took the Speaker's position, maintaining secrecy after congressional notification would not just be hard: it would be impossible.[36] There would be a direct conflict between notification and the country's ability to do anything covertly. That is one reason—however important reporting and consultation may be—why the final decision about when to notify Congress about unusually sensitive cases is a decision that must ultimately rest with the president.

The Constitutional Balance. On one side of the scale, we see from the Canadian example and from the problem of leaks that the president's implied power to withhold notification may, in rare and extraordinary cases, be a necessary adjunct to the inherent power to act. What is on Congress's side of the constitutional scale to warrant notification within forty-eight hours, without any exceptions? The best argument, to quote the Senate intelligence committee's 1988 report, is that notification is needed "to provide Congress with an opportunity to exercise its responsibilities under the Constitution."[37] The problem is that no legislative power requires notification under all conditions during any precisely specified period. All Congress needs to know is whether to continue funding continuing operations. We have had that information in every case except President Carter's and President Reagan's hostage-related Iran initiatives.

I suppose one could argue that failure to notify might, in the extreme, deprive us of our ability to decide about continuing to fund a particular operation. Iran-contra was such an extreme. But the choice is not one-sided. The price of ensuring notification about all operations within a specified time is to make some potentially lifesaving operations impossible. On the scale of risks, I am more concerned about depriving the president of his ability to act than I am about Congress's alleged inability to respond. I feel this way not because I am sanguine about every decision presidents might take. Rather, it is because I am confident Congress will eventually find out in this leaky city about decisions of any consequence. When that happens, Congress has the political tools to retaliate against any president who it feels withheld information without adequate justification. President Reagan learned this dramatically in the Iran-contra affair. It is a lesson no future president is likely to forget.

The Underlying Issue—Substitution for Public Debate. Underlying the dispute over notification is a more basic issue. Congress insists on notification because the executive's consultations with the intelligence committees substitute for the open debate and deliberation available in other policy arenas. The committees thus serve as a forum for mediating the tension between the Constitution's two-sided concern for security and informed consent. On the whole, the committees are not simply barriers for presidents to overcome. They can help presidents earn needed political support when the normal public tools cannot be used.

What happens, however, if some members think a particular operation is a bad idea? Sometimes the committee can persuade the executive branch to change its mind. But what if persuasion does not work? One answer offered by some of my colleagues is that no covert action should be undertaken unless it is supported by a bipartisan consensus. It is a good idea to begin from a presumption in favor of

116

bipartisanship, but wishing for consensus provides no guidance about how to behave when there are real disagreements. To insist on consensus as a precondition for action is equivalent to saying the president should not do anything controversial. In effect, it is equivalent to taking the president's power and giving it to Congress. In fact, demanding consensus could be worse than requiring an up-or-down vote. If it were taken seriously, the president would need the support of a supermajority before he could do anything. He might even need unanimity, if more members came to accept the view that leaking is legitimate. A consensus requirement, therefore, would be a decision rule weighted heavily toward the inaction side of any action-versus-inaction dispute. In the real world of breaking events, it is important to recognize that inaction is a form of action or decision.

To require or expect a consensus before action, in other words, is only one possible answer to questions that should be articulated more clearly and openly. Some of the questions are these: Who should hold what levers at what stage of the process? Under what political and legislative conditions should the presumption be weighted toward the president or toward Congress? That is, what rules should decide who prevails under conditions of stalemate? These questions apply not only to covert operations but to national security more generally. To broaden the discussion, therefore, I turn now to the War Powers Act.

War Powers

Like the proposed forty-eight-hour bill, the War Powers Act is a classic example of the problems with "never again" legislation.[38] The act was written to ensure that the United States would never again be drawn into a war without a congressional declaration authorizing U.S. participation. (Let us put aside, for the moment, the historical fact that the Gulf of Tonkin Resolution, authorizing the Vietnam War, would clearly have satisfied the terms of the War Powers Act.) The main "teeth" consist of four provisions: (1) The president is required to submit a report to the Speaker of the House and the president pro tempore of the Senate within forty-eight hours, describing the reasons for introducing U.S. armed forces into hostilities or into situations in which imminent involvement in hostilities is clearly indicated by the circumstances or under certain other conditions. (2) The president is required to terminate the involvement of U.S. forces within sixty calendar days unless Congress declares war or extends the period. (3) Congress may require the president to withdraw U.S. forces at any time by passing a concurrent resolution—a form of congressional action that does not require a presidential signature. (4)

117

Neither appropriations acts nor treaties count as congressional authorizations to use force, even if the use of force is clearly required by the terms of a previously ratified treaty.

The third provision needs little discussion because it involves a legislative veto of the sort the Supreme Court declared unconstitutional in 1983.[39] The others have never been tested authoritatively in court, but the entire framework strikes me as being unworkable and of dubious constitutionality. The War Powers Act explicitly states in public law that the president may not constitutionally use force without a formal declaration of war or statutory authorization unless the country is under attack.[40] Only on this assumption does the act's most essential feature—its use of the clock—make any sense. In the view of the act's main sponsors, the sixty-day clock was granting the president authority that it was fully within Congress's constitutional power to withhold. That authority was set to expire after two months because that should be enough time for Congress to reauthorize. If Congress fails to reauthorize, the sponsors concluded, the Constitution requires withdrawal because the president has no independent authority to act without Congress.[41]

I cannot accept such a limited view of the president's inherent constitutional powers. When the Constitutional Convention debated the war power on August 17, 1787, it decided to change draft language that would have given Congress the power to make war to the power to declare war. James Madison and Elbridge Gerry defended the change in the congressional power by saying it was necessary for "leaving the Executive the power to repel sudden attacks." Because of this statement, the advocates of a weak executive have claimed that the convention intended to limit the president's inherent power to that situation. What these advocates fail to note, however, is that in the very next speech of the same debate, Roger Sherman said that the new language giving Congress only the power to declare war would mean that the president would have the power "to commence war" and not simply defend against invasion.[42] Sherman's interpretation cannot be accepted as if it were definitive, but neither should Madison's or Gerry's. There was obviously an argument on the issue, and Madison's notes were sketchy, as they were so often in the convention's later stages. What we are left with is a clause in need of interpretation. On this score, the interpretation of history must at least bear some weight. From the earliest years presidents have deployed force without statutory authorization for purposes well beyond a defense against sudden attacks.[43]

I believe the Constitution gives the president not only the power but the obligation to protect American lives, to enforce valid treaties, and to defend other vital national interests. But the precise boundary of the president's inherent power is not crucial to my argument. Once one accepts the idea that there is any inherent presidential power to act, the framework of the War Powers Act collapses of its own weight. Congress cannot constitutionally set up a framework that declares an inherent presidential power inoperative after a specific date. Whatever the boundary, if the president's power to act comes directly from the Constitution and not from Congress, then the conditions that make an action valid on the first day of a crisis would make the same action equally valid on the sixty-first day if they have not changed. But if the conditions justifying the exercise of an inherent presidential power should disappear, the exercise would have no basis for continuing. What control are the conditions, not the time.

I promised earlier, however, that I would not let my argument rest solely on legal abstractions. If the United States must use force for an extended period, it would clearly be better for the country if the president were to show the world that he had support for what he was doing. Unfortunately, the War Powers Act seems to make effective interbranch cooperation more difficult instead of less. It grates against the underlying logic of the separation of powers and brings Congress's institutional proclivities to bear in exactly the ways the framers understood would be harmful. Meanwhile, adversaries know that instead of negotiating, they should wait us out for sixty days to see if we are serious.

The practical problem grows out of the way Congress works. By forcing a withdrawal in the absence of a specific congressional authorization, the act gives the political advantage to those members who oppose the president. Because bills must go through a multistage process—House committee, House floor, Senate committee, Senate floor, conference committee, and then back to the House floor and Senate floor—it is always easier for opponents to derail a controversial bill than for supporters to pass it. The War Powers Act tries to get around this with expedited procedures to guarantee an initial House and Senate vote within a prescribed period. But one vote cannot ensure that Congress will reach a conclusion. Because the act rests on the assumption that the power at issue comes from Congress, it preserves the constitutional right of both chambers to amend whatever resolution it may choose to discuss. As a result the act, in principle, cannot ensure an agreement between the two chambers. That is more than enough of a wedge for a determined set of opponents or fence straddlers.

The opponents and fence straddlers will also be helped by Congress's ingrained habits. Several recent studies of the act have shown that Congress typically tries to avoid responsibility for a clear decision, avoids confrontation when presidents refuse to invoke the act's terms, and prefers instead to praise successful presidential actions or criticize unsuccessful ones after the fact.[44] In 1987, for example, the Senate spent a long time debating whether the War Powers Act should have been triggered by the president's decision to have the U.S. Navy escort reflagged Kuwaiti oil tankers in the Persian Gulf. The net result was a resolution that did nothing more than promise a future debate and decision. When it became apparent in 1988 that the president's policy was bearing positive fruit—largely because our allies and the gulf countries finally became convinced that we were not going to cut and run—the issue was dropped.

Supporters of the War Powers Act say that the Senate's nondecision was possible only because President Reagan, like all his predecessors, refused to submit the kind of report that would have triggered an expedited vote. But who can have any doubt that, after debates over the order of battle and after the Senate's final action, a formal use of the act would probably have produced only a short-term extension of the deadline to allow more second-guessing in the next round? Formally invoking the act would not have changed the political realities and therefore would not have been likely to change the result.

Because Congress so often prefers to delay, the basic question becomes clearer. The root question about war powers is not about the desirability of consultation, deliberation, or congressional debates over resolutions. The more basic question, as I said in connection with intelligence oversight, is about finding an appropriate balance that will encourage deliberation without destroying the ability to act. I am firmly convinced that Congress would be no less likely to deliberate if there were no War Powers Act. The absence of a sixty-day crutch would be more likely to force Congress to find a common denominator with the president. Meanwhile, as Congress goes through its normal bargaining gyrations, the nation's adversaries would at least be aware that the country's highest elected official is empowered to maintain a predictable course.

The War Powers Act should therefore be repealed. The idea of a ticking clock is based on wrongheaded constitutional assumptions that produce mischievous and dangerous results. Congress has plenty of constitutional and political power to stop a president whenever it wants to. Anyone who doubts this should look at the long list of foreign policy limitation amendments to the appropriations acts of the past decade. If Congress does not have the will to support or oppose the president definitively, the nation should not be paralyzed by Congress's indecision.

Conclusion

At its best Congress is a deliberative body whose internal checks and balances favor delay as a method of stimulating compromise. At its worst it is a collection of 535 individual, separately elected politicians, each of whom seeks to claim credit and avoid blame. Whichever of these faces Congress may put on at any given moment, the legislative branch is ill equipped to handle many of the foreign policy tasks it has been taking upon itself lately.

It would be appropriate to end this discussion by going back to some beginnings. The purpose of the U.S. Constitution is to protect and promote liberty. But protecting liberty has at least two facets. In domestic policy it has to do with ensuring that proposed changes in law receive a proper airing to guard against minority or majority factional tyranny. The emphasis, therefore, is on forcing compromise and coalition, with the constitutional preference—albeit not always the practice—weighted toward inaction until compromise has been achieved.

The other aspect of liberty has to do with preservation and protection. According to the Declaration of Independence, governments are instituted not to create rights (which are "unalienable") but to secure them. Securing rights means, among other things, preserving the government's ability to respond internationally to countries that may want to harm us. In the face of danger, a tilt toward inaction would have just the opposite effect from a tilt toward inaction in domestic law. Instead of helping secure our liberty, it would help those foreign powers who want to endanger it. That is why the Constitution allowed a much greater scope for executive power in foreign than in domestic policy.

Underlying all this was the framers' hardheaded view of the tough world of international politics. They saw a world, much like today's, in which at least some states would work actively against our interests. They saw a world in which we would have adversarial relationships as well as friendly ones, a world in which force might have to buttress reason, a world in which there would always be some nation eager to exploit an inability to respond. Their world was different from ours in some important ways. Technology has shrunk the globe, making the need for quick response and predictability of purpose that much more important. But the fundamentals of human nature—from the motives of sovereign states to the proclivities of domestic politicians—remain unchanged. We would do well, therefore, to reinvigorate the framers' understanding of the separation of powers as we head toward the twenty-first century.

Notes

Chapter 1: Making Foreign Policy—The View from 1787

1. This essay relies significantly on material presented in Jack N. Rakove, "Solving a Constitutional Puzzle: The Treatymaking Clause as a Case Study," *Perspectives in American History*, n.s., vol. 1 (1984), pp. 233–81. I am grateful to the editors of that journal for allowing me to draw on that work. Readers interested in a fuller analysis of the evidence and further documentation as well as more sustained reflections on the enterprise of recovering the "original meaning" of the Constitution should consult the longer essay.

2. Max Farrand, ed., *The Records of the Federal Convention of 1787*, 2d rev. ed. (New Haven, Conn.: Yale University Press, 1987), vol. 1, pp. 423–24.

3. For a more thorough discussion of the points raised in the succeeding paragraphs, see Jack N. Rakove, *The Beginnings of National Politics: An Interpretive History of the Continental Congress* (New York: Knopf, 1979), pp. 342–52; and, more generally, Frederick W. Marks III, *Independence on Trial: Foreign Affairs and the Making of the Constitution* (Baton Rouge: Louisiana State University Press, 1973), pp. 3–95.

4. The relevant documents, including counsel Alexander Hamilton's extensive notes, are reprinted in Julius Goebel, Jr., ed., *The Law Practice of Alexander Hamilton: Documents and Commentary* (New York: Columbia University Press, 1964), vol. 1.

5. For this dispute and its political consequences, see Rakove, *Beginnings of National Politics*, pp. 243–74.

6. Jay to Jefferson, August 18, 1786, in Henry P. Johnston, ed., *The Correspondence and Public Papers of John Jay* (New York, 1890–1893), vol. 3, p. 210.

7. There are, of course, a number of other provisions that relate to foreign policy and national security concerns, broadly defined, which are not examined here. On most of these other questions, I find myself in close agreement with the positions taken in Charles A. Lofgren, *"Government from Reflection and Choice": Constitutional Essays on War, Foreign Relations, and Federalism* (New York: Oxford University Press, 1979). Also deserving of mention are two scrupulous analyses by the constitutional historian Arthur Bestor, Jr.: "Separation of Powers in the Domain of Foreign Affairs," *Seton Hall Law Review*, vol. 5 (1974), pp. 527–665; and "Respective Roles of Senate and President in the Making and Abrogation of Treaties," *Washington Law Review*, vol. 55 (1979), pp. 1–135.

8. Farrand, *Records,* vol. 1, pp. 64–66, 70, 73–74.

9. Thomas Burke to the North Carolina Assembly (August 1779), in Edmund C. Burnett, ed., *Letters of Members of the Continental Congress, 1774–1789* (Washington, D.C.: Carnegie Institute, 1921–1936), vol. 4, pp. 367–68; "Grotius," *Boston American Herald,* February 10, 1783; and "Solicitor," *New Hampshire Gazette,* November 15, 1783. See the discussion in Rakove, *Beginnings of National Politics,* pp. 383–85; and for a more extensive analysis of the equation between crown and Congress, Jerrilyn Greene Marston, *King and Congress: The Transfer of Political Legitimacy, 1774–1776* (Princeton, N.J.: Princeton University Press, 1987).

10. Madison to Caleb Wallace, August 23, 1785, in Robert A. Rutland et al., eds., *The Papers of James Madison* (Chicago: University of Chicago Press; and Charlottesville: University of Virginia Press, 1962–), vol. 8, pp. 352–53.

11. Farrand, *Records,* vol. 1, pp. 64–65.

12. Ibid., vol. 2, pp. 183, 185.

13. This view of congressional politics is developed more fully in Rakove, *Beginnings of National Politics,* esp. chaps. 5, 6, 11.

14. This point is particularly stressed in Bestor, "Respective Roles of Senate and President," pp. 88, 108–9.

15. Farrand, *Records,* vol. 1, p. 490; the larger issue of representation is discussed in Jack N. Rakove, "The Great Compromise: Ideas, Interests, and the Politics of Constitution-Making," *William and Mary Quarterly,* 3d ser., vol. 44 (1987), pp. 424–57.

16. For quotations in this and the next two paragraphs, see Farrand, *Records,* vol. 2, pp. 392–95.

17. Ibid., pp. 473, 481.

18. Jonathan Elliot, ed., *The Debates in the Several State Conventions, on the Adoption of the Federal Constitution* (Washington, D.C., 1854), vol. 4, pp. 263–65, 280–81.

19. The report of September 4 and the debates on the electoral college can be found in Farrand, *Records,* vol. 2, pp. 493–531; quotations at pp. 513, 523–24.

20. Ibid., p. 527. The assumption was that the large states would have the advantage in putting candidates forward, the small states in making the final determination among the leaders in the balloting in the electoral college.

21. The debates of September 7–8 are ibid., pp. 538–50; and cf. the draft of a motion that Madison apparently prepared but did not submit, which would have required the concurrence of the House of Representatives in any treaty "by which the territorial boundaries of the U.S. may be contracted, or by which the common rights of *navigation* or *fishery* . . . may be abridged"; James H. Hutson, ed., *Supplement to Max Farrand's The Records of the Federal Convention of 1787* (New Haven, Conn.: Yale University Press, 1987), p. 262.

22. Farrand, *Records,* vol. 2, p. 540.

23. Ibid., pp. 540–41.

24. Ibid., pp. 547–50.

25. Bestor, "Respective Roles of Senate and President," pp. 108–9.

26. Merrill Jensen et al., eds., *The Documentary History of the Ratification of*

the Constitution (Madison, Wis.: Historical Society of Wisconsin, 1976–), vol. 2, pp. 480, 491.

27. For representative comments, see Elliot, *Debates*, vol. 2, p. 460; vol. 3, pp. 221, 499–502; vol. 4, pp. 116, 124–25; and see the discussion in Rakove, "Solving a Constitutional Puzzle," pp. 251–53.

28. Alexander Hamilton, James Madison, and John Jay, *The Federalist*, ed. Benjamin F. Wright (Cambridge, Mass.: Belknap Press of Harvard University Press, 1961), pp. 420–25.

29. Ibid., pp. 475–80. Hamilton's treatment of treaty making as "a distinct department" of government suggests—but is not quite identical with—John Locke's classification of "federative" power as the third element in his trinity of separated powers. See Peter Laslett, ed., *John Locke's Two Treatises of Government: A Critical Edition with an Introduction and Apparatus Criticus* (Cambridge: Cambridge University Press, 1960), pp. 383–84.

30. See, for example, the remarks of William Davie (a framer who had, however, left the Philadelphia convention in mid-August) in the first North Carolina ratification convention; Elliot, *Debates*, vol. 4, pp. 119–20.

31. Madison to Jefferson, May 13, 1798, in *Letters and Other Writings of James Madison*, Congress ed. (Philadelphia: Lippincott, 1865), vol. 2, pp. 140–41.

CHAPTER 2: PRINCIPLE, PRUDENCE, AND THE CONSTITUTIONAL DIVISION
OF FOREIGN POLICY

1. John Locke, *Two Treatises of Government*, ed. Peter Laslett (New York: New American Library, 1965), II, sec. 3. The section of this essay on Locke is indebted to a suggestion from Robert A. Goldwin. The whole profited from the assistance of Alice Parker, who corrected several errors and made useful suggestions.

2. Ibid., II, sec. 87; see also secs. 124–26, 171.

3. Ibid., II, sec. 88.

4. Ibid.

5. Ibid., II, sec. 159.

6. Ibid., II, sec. 131.

7. Ibid., II, sec. 145.

8. Ibid., II, secs. 7–12, 16–17, 87, 127–28.

9. Ibid., II, secs. 129–30.

10. Ibid., II, secs. 128, 7.

11. Ibid., II, secs. 6, 124.

12. Ibid., II, secs. 125–26, 136.

13. Ibid., I, secs. 58, 86, 101; II secs. 6, 57.

14. Ibid., II, secs. 16, 135, 182.

15. Ibid., II, secs. 12, 135.

16. Locke, *Some Thoughts Concerning Education*, sec. 116, in James L. Axtell, ed., *The Educational Writings of John Locke* (Cambridge: Cambridge University Press, 1968), p. 226.

17. Locke, *Two Treatises*, II, secs. 146, 108, 88.

18. Ibid., II, sec. 147.

19. Ibid.

20. Ibid., II, secs. 22, 88, 94, 136–37.

21. Ibid., II, secs. 134, 149–50, 153, 243.

22. Ibid., II, sec. 150.

23. Ibid., II, sec. 153.

24. Ibid., II, sec. 139.

25. Ibid., II, sec. 148.

26. Ibid., II, secs. 151–52.

27. Ibid., II, sec. 14, chap. 16.

28. Locke, "Some Thoughts Concerning Reading and Study for a Gentleman," in *Educational Writings*, p. 400.

29. Locke, *Some Thoughts Concerning Education*, sec. 186, pp. 294–95.

30. Locke, *Two Treatises*, II, sec. 134; see also secs. 149, 159.

31. See Nathan Tarcov, "Principle and Prudence in Foreign Policy: The Founders' Perspective," *The Public Interest* 76 (Summer 1984), pp. 45–60.

32. Alexander Hamilton, James Madison, and John Jay, *The Federalist Papers*, ed. Clinton Rossiter (New York: New American Library, 1961), No. 3, p. 42.

33. For the meaning for the founding generation of the distinction between just and unjust wars, see Reginald C. Stuart, *War and American Thought: From the Revolution to the Monroe Doctrine* (Kent, Ohio: Kent State University Press, 1982), pp. 6–11, 17–24.

34. Ibid., No. 3, p. 42.

35. *The Federalist Papers*, No. 3, p. 42.

36. Compare the parallel conduct of Madison in No. 63, p. 384 ("To a people as little blinded by prejudice or corrupted by flattery as those whom I address . . .") and Hamilton in No. 71, p. 432 ("their good sense would despise the adulator who should pretend . . .").

37. Ibid., No. 4, p. 49.

38. Ibid., No. 3, pp. 42–43.

39. Compare Garry Wills, *Explaining America: The Federalist* (Garden City, N.Y.: Doubleday, 1981), pp. 249–53. Stephen P. Rosen points out, however, that the argument may not apply as well in Jay's case as in Madison's, "Leadership in American Foreign Policy: The Problem of War and Republican Government" (Ph.D. diss., Harvard University 1979), pp. 20–23.

40. *The Federalist Papers*, No. 3, pp. 43–45.

41. Ibid., No. 3, p. 44; No. 15, p. 106.

42. Ibid., No. 3, p. 45.

43. Ibid., No. 4, p. 46.

44. Ibid.

45. Ibid., pp. 46–47.

46. Ibid., p. 47.

47. See *Brutus* No. 7, No. 10, and Patrick Henry in *The Complete Anti-Federalist*, ed. Herbert J. Storing (Chicago: University of Chicago Press, 1981), 2.9.86–87, 2.9.119, 5.16.2.

48. See David F. Epstein, *The Political Theory of The Federalist* (Chicago: University of Chicago Press, 1984), p. 27.

49. *The Federalist Papers*, No. 5, p. 51.

50. See Epstein, *Political Theory of The Federalist*, pp. 40–50.

51. *The Federalist Papers*, No. 23, pp. 153–54.

52. Ibid., No. 31, pp. 194–95.

53. Ibid., No. 30, p. 190.

54. Ibid., pp. 191–93.

55. Ibid., No. 34, pp. 208–9.

56. Ibid., No. 36, p. 223.

57. Ibid., No. 41, p. 257.

58. Ibid., No. 26, p. 173; No. 25, pp. 165–66.

59. Ibid., Nos. 62–64.

60. Ibid., Nos. 64, 70, 75.

CHAPTER 3: REFLECTIONS ON THE ROLE OF THE JUDICIARY IN FOREIGN POLICY

1. Edward S. Corwin, *The President: Office and Powers*, 4th rev. ed. (New York: New York University Press, 1957), p. 170.

2. The best books of recent years are Abraham Sofaer, *War, Foreign Affairs and Constitutional Power* (Cambridge, Mass.: Ballinger,1976), and Louis Henkin, *Foreign Affairs and the Constitution* (New York: Norton, 1972).

3. Hamilton wrote under the name of Pacificus, Madison under the name of Helvidius, in a series of articles in *The Gazette of the United States*. The exchange is succinctly summarized by Corwin, *The President*, pp. 178–82.

4. "Nobody answers him and his doctrines are taken for confessed. For God's sake, my dear Sir, take up your pen, select the most striking heresies and cut him to pieces in face of the public." Cited by Corwin, ibid., p. 180.

5. Youngstown Sheet & Tube Co. v. Sawyer, 343 U.S. 579, 634 (1952). While serving as attorney general, however, Jackson evinced no such difficulty. See Alfred H. Kelly, Winfred A. Harbison, and Herman Belz, *The American Constitution: Its Origins and Development*, 6th ed. (New York: Norton, 1982), pp. 552–58.

6. Tocqueville, *Democracy in America*, edited by J. P. Mayer and Max Lerner (New York: Harper & Row, 1966), p. 248. See also chap. 6, "Judicial Power in the United States and Its Effect on Political Society."

7. Marbury v. Madison, 5 U.S. 137, 177 (1803).

8. Alexander Bickel, *The Least Dangerous Branch* (Indianapolis: Bobbs-Merrill, 1962), p. 184.

9. Foster v. Neilson, 27 U.S. 332 (1924).

10. Asakura v. Seattle, 265 U.S. 332 (1924); Missouri v. Holland, 252 U.S. 416 (1920).

11. U.S. v. Pink, 315 U.S. 203 (1942); U.S. v. Guy W. Capps, Inc., 204 F.2d 655 (4th Cir. 1953), aff'd. on other grounds 348 U.S. 296 (1955).

12. Reid v. Covert, 354 U.S. 1 (1957).

13. U.S. v. Pink; U.S. v. Belmont, 301 U.S. 324 (1937).

14. U.S. Constitution, Article III, section 2; Article VI.

15. Congressional Research Service, Library of Congress, *The Constitution of the United States of America: Analysis and Interpretation*, 1982 ed. (Washington, D.C.: Government Printing Office), p. 505.

16. "It has also been suggested that the prohibitions against governmental action contained in the Constitution—the Bill of Rights particularly—limit the exercise of the treaty power. No doubt this is true, though again there are no cases which so hold." Ibid., p. 513.

17. Goldwater v. Carter, 444 U.S. 996 (1979).

18. Baker v. Carr, 369 U.S. 186, 211 (1962).

19. Haig v. Agee, 453 U.S. 280, 292 (1981).

20. Charles A. Lofgren, *Government from Reflection and Choice* (New York: Oxford University Press, 1986), p. 38.

21. 272 U.S. 52 (1926).

22. Ibid., at 118.

23. 299 U.S. 304 (1936).

24. Ibid., at 319.

25. Ibid., at 319–20.

26. Lofgren, *Government*, pp. 167–205; Raoul Berger, "The Presidential Monopoly of Foreign Relations," *Michigan Law Review*, vol. 71 (1972), p. 1; Sar Levitan, "The Foreign Relations Power: An Analysis of Mr. Justice Sutherland's Theory," *Yale Law Journal*, vol. 55 (1946), p. 467.

27. Lofgren, *Government*, pp. 170–73.

28. Kelly, Harbison, and Belz, *The American Constitution*, p. 553.

29. Youngstown Sheet & Tube Co. v. Sawyer, 343 U.S. 579 (1952).

30. Ibid., at 583–84.

31. Ibid., at 657.

32. For contrasting views, see Laurence H. Tribe, *American Constitutional Law* (Mincola, N.Y.: Foundation Press, 1978), pp. 56–92; Bickel, *Least Dangerous Branch*, pp. 23–28, 69–71, 183–98.

33. Marbury v. Madison, 5 U.S. 137, 165–66 (1803).

34. See, for example, Oetjen v. Central Leather Co., 246 U.S. 297 (1918); Jones v. United States, 137 U.S. 202 (1890).

35. See Goldwater v. Carter, 444 U.S. 996 (1979); Atlee v. Richardson, 411 U.S. 911 (1973).

36. Goldwater v. Carter, at 1002.

37. Ibid.

38. See, for example, Jesse Choper, *Judicial Review and the National Political Process* (Chicago: University of Chicago Press, 1980).

39. See, for example, L. Gordon Crovitz and Jeremy A. Rabkin, eds., *The Fettered Presidency* (Washington, D.C.: American Enterprise Institute, 1989).

40. Lowry v. Reagan, 676 F.Supp. 333 (D.D.C. 1987).

41. Ibid., at 339 (citations omitted).

42. Ibid. Compare Robert H. Bork, "Foreword," in *Fettered Presidency*, p. xii.

43. Lowry v. Reagan, at 340–41.

44. Tocqueville, *Democracy in America*, pp. 136–37.

CHAPTER 4: FOREIGN TRADE AND THE CONSTITUTION

1. Quoted in Jeffrey H. Birnbaum, "President Reagan Signs Big Trade Bill, but Signals He May Ignore Parts of It," *Wall Street Journal*, August 24, 1988, p. 40. President Reagan criticized the bill's provisions that strongly "directed"

the executive branch to negotiate with foreign countries on certain trade issues and to conduct trade investigations at the urging of individual congressional committees. Other provisions shift responsibility for certain decisions from the president to the U.S. trade representative, a member of the president's cabinet.

2. Raymond J. Ahearn and Alfred Reifman, "Trade Legislation in 1987: Congress Takes Charge," *National Bureau of Economic Research Paper on Trade Policy and the Congress*, 1987, p. 7. On April 27, 1987, twelve cabinet members wrote to House Speaker James Wright and on June 22, 1987, fourteen cabinet members wrote to Senate Majority Leader Robert Byrd joint letters that contained a summary of the administration's concerns about the substance of the House and Senate versions of the trade bill (unpublished letters).

3. "Remarks by the President to Business Leaders and Members of the President's Export Council and Advisory Committee for Trade Negotiations," East Room, White House, September 23, 1985 (unpublished), p. 3.

4. *Congressional Record*, July 21, 1987, p. S10296.

5. For a discussion of the War Powers Resolution, see Jacob K. Javits, *Javits: The Autobiography of a Public Man* (Boston: Houghton Mifflin Co., 1981), pp. 393–414.

6. For example, the Supreme Court in Field v. Clark (1891) upheld Congress's right to invest the president with "large discretion in matters arising out of the execution of statutes relating to trade and commerce with other nations," and in FEA v. Algonquin SNG Inc. (1976) it upheld the wide delegation given to the president in the Trade Expansion Act of 1962 to "take such action and for such time, as he deemed necessary to adjust the imports" of a product that threatens national security. See Louis Fisher, *Constitutional Conflicts between Congress and the President* (Princeton, N.J.: Princeton University Press, 1985).

7. *Report of the Committee on Ways and Means, U.S. House of Representatives, to Accompany H.R. #3, the Trade and International Economic Policy Reform Act of 1987*, Report 100-40, pt. 1, p. 2.

8. In addition, Congress uses the delegating legislation to make changes in the remedies found in U.S. trade law that are available to U.S. industry to deal with unfairly traded or injurious imports (for example, countervailing or antidumping duty laws) or to open foreign markets (for example, section 301 trade proceedings). The increasing use of such remedies by industry to deal with trade, competitiveness, and other macroeconomic problems faced by the United States has led Thomas R. Howell and Alan W. Wolf to express their concern "that to a degree unmatched in other nations, trade law is not merely an important aspect of U.S. trade policy—it actually *is* trade policy." "The Role of Trade Law in the Making of Trade Policy," in John H. Jackson et al., eds., *International Trade Policy: The Lawyer's Perspective* (New York: Matthew Bender, 1985), pp. 3–21.

9. Congress does not have a similar direct final say in foreign policy. Whereas Congress can always return to legislation that is directly related to trade policy, it has only the indirect control over the purse to control foreign policy.

10. Observation made by Representative John J. Duncan during the House

debate on the 1988 trade bill, *Congressional Record*, April 28, 1987, p. H2557.

11. Louis Henkin, *Foreign Affairs and the Constitution* (Mineola, N.Y.: Foundation Press, 1972), p. 33.

12. Frederick W. Marks III, *Independence on Trial: Foreign Affairs and the Making of the Constitution* (Wilmington, Del.: Scholarly Resources, 1986), p. 80. The chapter's discussion of the pre-1789 influences on the commerce clause is drawn from Marks.

13. Quoted ibid., p. 66.

14. Quoted ibid., p. 84.

15. Ibid., pp. 85–91.

16. James Madison, *Federalist* No. 45.

17. Madison, *Federalist* No. 42.

18. Alexander Hamilton, *Federalist* No. 69.

19. Louis Fisher, *President and Congress: Power and Policy* (New York: Free Press, 1972), pp. 58–60.

20. Ibid., p. 135.

21. Quoted in Robert Pastor, "The Cry-and-Sigh Syndrome: Congress and Trade Policy," in Allen Schick, ed., *Making Economic Policy in Congress* (Washington, D.C.: American Enterprise Institute, 1983), p. 163.

22. Neither the House Ways and Means Committee nor the Senate Finance Committee debated tariffs on individual products during consideration of the 1934 bill.

23. Pastor, "Cry-and-Sigh Syndrome," p. 165.

24. Raymond J. Ahearn, *Trade Conflict in the 99th Congress* (Washington, D.C.: Congressional Research Service, 1987), p. 8.

25. NTBs are either border measures that are intended to affect international trade directly (quotas, export subsidies) or domestic measures, such as health and safety standards and government procurement regulations, that indirectly distort international trade.

26. The "democratic dilemma" refers to the ability of legislative bodies with their inherent decentralized authority and openness to play a role in the execution of foreign policy, which puts a premium on speed, decisiveness, and—quite often—secrecy. For a general discussion of the democratic dilemma, see I. M. Destler, "Trade Consensus, SALT Stalemate: Congress and Foreign Policy in the 1970s," in Thomas E. Mann and Norman J. Ornstein, eds., *The New Congress* (Washington, D.C.: American Enterprise Institute, 1981), pp. 329–33.

27. This paper does not deal with the substance of U.S. trade policy, including the policy directives on negotiating objectives, changes in U.S. laws on unfair trading practices, measures to open foreign markets to U.S. exports, or the changes in the domestic administration of U.S. trade laws that were contained in the 1974 and 1988 trade bills.

28. Senators from oil-consuming states opposed an energy security amendment in the Senate version of the 1988 trade bill on "constitutional grounds." The constitutional issue involved was, however, not over trade policy but over the unlimited delegation to the president of legislative power "previously reserved to and exercised by Congress," which represented "vir-

tual abrogation of congressional prerogatives and responsibilities in the legislative process." "Additional Views of Senator Bob Packwood," *Report of the Committee on Finance, United States Senate, on S.490, Omnibus Trade Act of 1987, Together with Additional Views*, Report 100-71, p. 262. Hereafter cited as *Finance Committee Report*.

29. *Congressional Record*, June 28, 1987, p. S8644.

30. Ibid., December 10, 1973, p. 10927.

31. Known as the Burke-Hartke bill, the draft legislation provided for widespread quantitative restrictions on U.S. imports and aimed at discouraging foreign investment by U.S. firms. See I. M. Destler, *Making of Foreign Economic Policy* (Washington, D.C.: Brookings Institution, 1980), p. 136.

32. *Congressional Record*, December 13, 1973, p. 12383.

33. Ibid., December 10, 1973, p. 10997.

34. Ibid., pp. 10957-59.

35. Ibid., June 26, 1987, pp. S8822-24.

36. Ibid., April 28, 1987, p. H2560.

37. Ibid., June 25, 1987, p. S8642.

38. *Finance Committee Report*, p. 5.

39. *Congressional Record*, June 25, 1987, p. S8654.

40. Ibid., p. S8677.

41. In 1983 the Supreme Court struck down the one-House veto (I.N.S. v. Chadha).

42. *Congressional Record*, December 10, 1973, p. 10954.

43. Pastor, "Cry-and-Sigh Syndrome," pp. 178-79.

44. *Congressional Record*, June 25, 1987, p. S8657.

45. "Administration Objections to and Comments on Senate Trade and Related Legislation," appended to the Administration Letter to Senate Majority Leader Byrd, June 22, 1987, p. 14.

46. President Reagan had threatened to veto the trade bill if a compromise could not be found on the Toshiba-Kongsberg sanctions and the foreign investment provisions.

47. Quoted in Destler, *Making of Foreign Economic Policy*, p. 178.

48. For a general review of international economic policy making in the United States, see Stephen D. Cohen, *The Making of United States International Economic Policy* (New York: Praeger, 1981).

49. In addition, the USTR must still submit an annual foreign barriers report, and the International Trade Commission continues to be required to submit a factual report on the operation of the trade agreements program. The USTR and other agencies are also required to file reports under the various fair trade provisions of the 1988 and earlier trade bills. The 1988 trade bill requires the executive branch to make more than eighty new reports to the full Congress or to specified congressional committees. See Simon M. Kriesberg and Eric R. Biel, *The Omnibus Trade and Competitiveness Act of 1988: New Reports Required of the Executive Branch* (Washington, D.C.: Mayer, Brown & Platt, 1988).

50. The bill changes the name of the Advisory Committee for Trade Negotiations, which is presidentially appointed and sits at the top of the private

sector advisory pyramid, to the Advisory Committee for Trade Policy and Negotiations.

51. *Annual Report of the President of the United States on the Trade Agreements Program, 1984–85* (Washington, D.C.: Office of the U.S. Trade Representative, 1986), p. 179.

52. *Congressional Record,* July 23, 1979, p. 20181.

53. Ibid., July 10, 1979, p. 17820.

54. Ibid., July 23, 1979, p. 20151.

55. Ibid., July 10, 1979, p. 17857.

56. Ibid., p. 20152.

57. In certain respects the 1979 Trade Agreements Act launched a new cycle, though mostly in the domestic area of countervailing and antidumping petitions. See, for example, the direction that Senator Danforth gave to policy in a colloquy with Senator Ribicoff on the legislative intent behind the antidumping and countervailing provisions of the act. *Congressional Record,* July 23, 1979, pp. 20171–72.

58. Henkin, *Foreign Affairs and the Constitution,* pp. 275–76.

CHAPTER 5: THE PROBLEM OF PRACTICE—FOREIGN POLICY AND THE CONSTITUTION

1. For more examples, and for discussion from different points of view of the themes I am exploring, see, among others: David Abshire, *Foreign Policy Makers: President vs. Congress* (Beverly Hills: Sage Publications, 1979); John C. Stennis and J. William Fulbright, *The Role of Congress in Foreign Policy* (Washington, D.C.: American Enterprise Institute, 1971); Morton Berkowitz, P. G. Bock, and Vincent J. Fuccillo, *The Politics of American Foreign Policy* (Englewood Cliffs: Prentice Hall, 1977); Richard Lugar, *Letters to the Next President* (New York: Simon and Schuster, 1988).

2. See Strobe Talbott, *Deadly Gambits* (New York: Knopf, 1984).

3. Consider Locke's *Second Treatise,* and *The Federalist Papers;* compare with Arthur M. Schlesinger, Jr., *The Imperial Presidency* (New York: Houghton Mifflin, 1973).

4. See Abraham Lincoln, "The Perpetuation of our Political Institutions," in Roy P. Basler, ed., *The Collected Works of Abraham Lincoln* (New Brunswick, N.J.: Rutgers University Press, 1953), vol. 1, pp. 108–15.

5. *Washington Post,* December 3, 1988.

CHAPTER 7: CONGRESSIONAL OVERREACHING IN FOREIGN POLICY

1. U.S. House of Representatives, Select Committee to Investigate Covert Arms Transactions with Iran, and U.S. Senate, Select Committee on Secret Military Assistance to Iran and the Nicaraguan Opposition, 100th Cong. 1st sess., *Report of the Congressional Committees Investigating the Iran-Contra Affair, with Supplemental, Minority, and Additional Views,* H.Rept. 100–433, S.Rept. 100–216 (Washington, D.C., 1987), *Minority Report,* chaps. 2–4, pp. 457–79. Hereafter cited as Iran-Contra Report.

2. This well-known phrase comes from Edward S. Corwin, *The President:*

Office and Powers (New York: New York University Press, 4th rev. ed., 1957), p. 171.

3. Alexander Hamilton, James Madison, and John Jay, *The Federalist,* ed. Jacob Cooke (Middletown, Conn.: Wesleyan University Press, 1961), No. 70, pp. 471–72.

4. "Contrary to the political maxim that power abhors a vacuum, it is simply *not* the case that powers removed or stripped away from one branch will find a home in another. Power can be dissipated and lost. There are some tasks that one branch can perform that others simply cannot." Caspar Weinberger, "Non-Partisan National Security Policy: History, War Powers, and the Persian Gulf," remarks prepared for delivery by Secretary of Defense Weinberger to the Naval Postgraduate School, Monterey, California, November 2, 1987, as printed in U.S. Department of Defense, News Release 564-87, of the same date.

5. John Felton, "Nicaragua Peace Process Moves to Capitol Hill," *Congressional Quarterly,* November 14, 1987, p. 2791.

6. Ibid., p. 2789.

7. Rowland Evans and Robert Novak, "Dash to Managua," *Washington Post,* May 15, 1985.

8. Letter from James Wright et al. to Commandante Daniel Ortega, March 20, 1984.

9. Letter from Ronald V. Dellums et al. to Prime Minister Wilfried Martens, January 11, 1985.

10. Rowland Evans and Robert Novak, "Message to Martens," *Washington Post,* February 6, 1985, p. A19.

11. John Felton, "Iran: Tensions Mount As Crisis Continues," *Congressional Quarterly,* December 1, 1979, p. 2704.

12. U.S. Congress, 100th Cong., 1st sess., Joint Hearings before the Senate Select Committee on Secret Military Assistance to Iran and the Nicaraguan Opposition and the House Select Committee to Investigate Covert Arms Transactions with Iran, *The Iran-Contra Investigation,* vol. 100-5, pp. 571–75. See also vol. 100-3, pp. 92, 387, and vol. 100-5, pp. 26–27.

13. 1 Stat. 613 (1799).

14. 18 U.S.C. 953.

15. Charles Warren (assistant attorney general), *History of Laws Prohibiting Correspondence with a Foreign Government and Acceptance of a Commission,* U.S. Senate, 64th Cong., 2d sess., S.Doc. 64-696 (1917), p. 7. See also, *Annals of Congress,* Fifth Cong., 3d sess. (Dec. 3, 1798–March 3, 1789), pp. 2487–2721.

16. See Iran-Contra Report, *Minority Report,* chap. 3, pp. 463–66, and chap. 4, pp. 472–73.

17. John Goshko, "Wright, in 'Good Faith,' Delays Legislation Requiring Fast Notice of Covert Acts," *Washington Post,* February 1, 1989; Bill Gertz, "House Won't Ask 48-Hour Disclosure of Covert Operations," *Washington Times,* February 1, 1989; and Michael Oreskes, "Wright, in Gesture to Bush, Shelves Bill on Covert Acts," *New York Times,* February 1, 1989.

18. Youngstown Sheet and Tube Co. v. Sawyer, 343 U.S. 579, 635–38 (1952).

19. Ibid. at 645.

20. For a summary, see Iran-Contra Report, pp. 467–69.

21. For a somewhat analogous but less absurd case, see Brown v. Califano, 627 F. 2d 1221 (1980).

22. Anderson v. Dunn, 6 Wheat. 204, 225–26 (1821).

23. Ibid. at 628–29.

24. Kilbourn v. Thompson, 103 U.S. 168 (1881), read the power narrowly, but McGrain v. Dougherty, 273 U.S. 135 (1927), and Sinclair v. U.S., 279 U.S. 263 (1929), read *Kilbourn* narrowly. Later cases have tended to involve conflicts between the contempt power and the First Amendment: Watkins v. U.S., 354 U.S. 178 (1957); and Barenblatt v. U.S., 360 U.S. 109 (1959).

25. U.S. v. Nixon, 418 U.S. 683 (1974).

26. U.S. House of Representatives, Permanent Select Committee on Intelligence, Subcommittee on Legislation, 100th Cong., 1st sess., *Hearings on H.R. 1013, H.R. 1371, and Other Proposals Which Address the Issue of Affording Prior Notice of Covert Actions to the Congress,* April 1 and 8, June 10, 1987, p. 45. See also pp. 46, 49, 58, 61.

27. Ibid., p. 158. See also: Letter from Secretary of Defense Frank Carlucci to David Boren, chairman of the Senate Select Committee on Intelligence, August 8, 1988.

28. It is worth emphasizing that the proposed bill would have required notification within forty-eight hours of an operation's start—that is, when the United States began putting people in place, not when the operation was finished.

29. Iran-Contra Report, *Minority Report,* chap. 13, pp. 575–80.

30. The Iran-contra minority report indicated two occasions when there were apparently inadvertent, unauthorized disclosures from past Senate committee members in this group of eight. Ibid., p. 577.

31. Jim Drinkard, "Wright Says CIA Operatives Aim at Provoking Sandinistas," Associated Press wire service, September 20, 1988; Joe Pichirallo, "CIA Attempted to Provoke Sandinistas, Wright Asserts," *Washington Post,* September 21, 1988, pp. A1, A28; Susan F. Rasky, "CIA Tied to Nicaragua Provocations," *New York Times,* September 21, 1988; and Bill Gertz and Peter LaBarbera, "Wright Draws Fire for Spilling Secrets," *Washington Times,* September 21, 1988, pp. A1, A11.

32. See also H.Res. 561, 100th Cong., 2d sess., filed September 30 by the six Republican members of the House Select Committee on Intelligence.

33. The Speaker resigned from Congress three months after the AEI conference, before the committee had completed its investigation.

34. Jim Drinkard, "Wright's Confident House Panels Will Drop Complaints about CIA Disclosures," Associated Press wire service, September 26, 1988; and Bill Gertz and Peter LaBarbera, "Congressmen Have Right to Reveal Secrets, Wright Says," *Washington Times,* September 27, 1988, p. A1.

35. (1) "The late Rep. Leo Ryan told me (in 1975) that he would condone such a leak if it was the only way to block an ill conceived operation." See Daniel Schorr, "Cloak and Dagger Relics," *Washington Post,* November 14, 1985, p. A23. (2) Senator Joseph Biden, then a member of the intelligence committee, told a reporter he had "twice threatened to go public with covert action plans by the Reagan Administration that were harebrained." See Brit Hume, "Mighty Mouth," *New Republic,* September 1, 1986, p. 20.

36. In the 1970s, when operations had to be reported to many more committees, William Colby, former director of central intelligence, said that "every new project submitted to this procedure leaked, and the 'covert' part of CIA's covert action seemed almost gone." See William Colby, *Honorable Men* (New York: Simon and Schuster, 1978), p. 423.

37. U.S. Senate, 100th Cong., 2d sess., Select Committee on Intelligence, *Intelligence Oversight Act of 1988*, S.Rept. 100-276 (Jan. 27, 1988), p. 21.

38. P.L. 93-148 [H.J.Res. 542], 87 Stat. 555, 50 U.S.C. 1541–48, passed over the president's veto November 7, 1973.

39. Immigration and Naturalization Service v. Chadha, 462 U.S. 919 (1983).

40. P.L. 93-148, sec. 2(c).

41. See, for example, U.S. Senate, Committee on Foreign Relations, 92d Cong., 2d sess., *War Powers*, S.Rept. 92-606, to accompany S.2956 (Feb. 9, 1972), pp. 4, 12.

42. Max Farrand, *The Records of the Federal Convention of 1787*, 4 vols. (New Haven, Conn.: Yale University Press, 1937), vol. 2, pp. 318–19.

43. See Abraham D. Sofaer, *War, Foreign Affairs, and Constitutional Power* (Cambridge, Mass.: Ballinger, 1976). See also J. T. Emerson, "War Powers Legislation," *West Virginia Law Review*, vol. 74 (1972), pp. 53, 88–119. Emerson's article ends with a long list of the occasions on which force was used without a declaration of war. A revised version of the list appears in U.S. House of Representatives, Committee on Foreign Affairs, 93d Cong., 1st sess., *War Powers*, Hearings before the Subcommittee on National Security Policy and Scientific Developments, Exhibit 2, pp. 328–76 (1973).

44. See Pat M. Holt, *The War Powers Resolution* (Washington, D.C.: American Enterprise Institute, 1978), p. 33; and Robert F. Turner, *The War Powers Resolution: Its Implementation in Theory and Practice* (Philadelphia: Foreign Policy Research Institute, 1983), pp. 119–25.

A NOTE ON THE BOOK

*This book was edited by the publications staff
of the American Enterprise Institute.
The text was set in Palatino, a typeface designed by Hermann Zapf.
Coghill Book Typesetting Company, of Richmond, Virginia,
set the type, and Edwards Brothers Incorporated,
of Ann Arbor, Michigan, printed and bound the book,
using permanent, acid-free paper.*

The AEI Press is the publisher for the American Enterprise Institute for Public Policy Research, 1150 Seventeenth Street, N.W., Washington, D.C. 20036: *Christopher C. DeMuth,* publisher; *Edward Styles,* director; *Dana Lane,* editor; *Ann Petty,* editor; *Andrea Posner,* editor; *Teresa Fung,* editorial assistant (rights and permissions). Books published by the AEI Press are distributed by arrangement with the University Press of America, 4720 Boston Way, Lanham, Md. 20706.